GAMES IN THE PLATFORM ECONOMY

Steam's Tangled Markets

Anne Mette Thorhauge

BRISTOL
UNIVERSITY
PRESS

First published in Great Britain in 2023 by

Bristol University Press
University of Bristol
1-9 Old Park Hill
Bristol
BS2 8BB
UK
t: +44 (0)117 374 6645
e: bup-info@bristol.ac.uk

Details of international sales and distribution partners are available at bristoluniversitypress.co.uk

British Library Cataloguing in Publication Data
A catalogue record for this book is available from the British Library

ISBN 978-1-5292-2304-0 hardcover
ISBN 978-1-5292-2305-7 ePub
ISBN 978-1-5292-2306-4 ePdf

Cover design: Lyn Davies Design
Front cover image: Alamy Stock Photo/Divina Epiphania
Bristol University Press uses environmentally responsible print partners.
Printed and bound in Great Britain by CPI Group (UK) Ltd, Croydon, CR0 4YY

FSC
www.fsc.org
MIX
Paper | Supporting responsible forestry
FSC® C013604

I dedicate this work to Mathilde, my oldest friend and life witness. You embarked on your irrevocable journey towards death about the time I embarked on the task of writing this book. Though it may not appear directly from the pages, my writing process and your early passing have been deeply intertwined. In my writing exiles, I have been occupied as much with our exchanges, the wordy and the wordless ones, as with the detached conversations of academic discourse. And though our encounters have now taken a silent and contemplative form, I keep you right here with me.

Contents

List of Figures and Table

Figures

Table

Acknowledgements

I could not have written this book without the help and support from dear colleagues, friends, and family. I would like to thank my reading group in economic sociology, Janus Hansen, Eva Iris Otto, Rasmus Munksgaard, Andreas Gregersen, and Jacob Ørmen, who have given important feedback at various stages of the analysis. Also, thank you to my colleagues in the Section of Digital Communication and the Centre for Tracking and Society at the University of Copenhagen for valuable feedback, not least Klaus Bruhn Jensen, who has been kind enough to give parts of the book a critical read. I would like to thank Paul Stevens, my editor, and Vincent Manzerolle for going through the first version of the manuscript, as well as David Nieborg for useful comments in the final stages of editing. Moreover, thanks go to Victor Kolind, Jacob Larsen, and Selda Eren Kanat, who have supported me in my ongoing effort to develop data collection tools suitable for the task at hand, and Ole Comoll who has provided visuals for the figures in Chapter 6. Finally, I would like to thank my husband and children, who have endured my occasional physical and mental absence throughout the writing process.

Introduction: Steam's Tangled Markets

In 2018, Valve Corporation, the owner of the Steam gaming platform, made a seemingly minor feature change. It involved that game items obtained in Steam-based games could only be traded between players after a waiting period of seven days after acquisition. This feature change, often referred to as 'the cooldown', cost the most active Steam traders several thousands of euros due to the subsequent plunge in market prices. It was implemented as a response to rising public concern regarding the proliferation of so-called skin trading and skin gambling on shady websites. In the time leading up to the event, several critical voices had accused Valve of profiting from illegal gambling with items from the Steam platform. ESPN.com stated that *Counter-Strike: Global Offensive*, one of Steam's most lucrative game titles, had 'spawned a wild multibillion-dollar world of online casino gambling; it's barely regulated and open to any kid who wants in',[1] and the Washington State Gambling Commission stated that Valve was 'responsible for the unregulated *Counter-Strike: Global Offensive* gambling that's gone on through Steam' and ordered Valve to take immediate action.[2] In the wake of these critiques, Valve was facing several lawsuits.

But how can a simple time delay cost ordinary users thousands of euros, and how can a simple feature change make a difference on seemingly unaffiliated websites? How is it even possible to gamble with items from Steam-based games? To understand these issues, one must understand the distinct features of the Steam platform economy and design, and how these frame economic practices beyond the platform. In this book, I will explain Steam as a 'tangled market', a set of interconnected and mutually dependent market contexts, that creates revenue from microtransactions through the strategic shaping of market interactions on and beyond the platform. Unlike other market platforms such as the App Store and Google Play, Steam does not offer entrepreneurs a system for generating revenue through advertising. Instead, it pushes its microtransaction system as a preferred alternative. And unlike other gaming platforms, Steam, to an unprecedented degree, integrates virtual economies and players' economic interaction in an effort to intensify and expand the quantity of economic transactions on the platform and let these practices develop beyond the platform. In this book, I will analyse how this business model is reflected in the continuous development of Steam's platform design, and how these designed affordances are transformed into business strategies by various actors operating on and beyond the platform. Moreover, I will argue that the integration of users as economic actors in the wider platform economy reflects an alternative approach to user commodification as compared to that of advertising, which may hint to future business models of Big Tech, addressing users simultaneously as consumers, creators, and traders in different contexts of the platform's tangled market. To conduct this analysis, I will apply an analytical framework based on insights from platform studies, the economic sociology of markets, and theories of user commodification. In the following sections, I will firstly present Steam's tangled market as my primary case of analysis. Secondly, I will present the key analytical concepts, including varying notions of platforms, player-driven economies, the (dis)embeddedness of economic action (Polanyi, 1944; Granovetter, 1985), and markets as fields of strategic action where incumbents and challengers maintain or challenge a given market order (Fligstein, 1996, 2001). Finally, I will discuss how this business strategy differs fundamentally from the predominantly advertisement-driven platforms of entertainment media and hence involves an alternative approach to user commodification in this domain.

Steam's tangled markets

The Steam platform simultaneously represents an 'outlier case' due to its innovative approach to the monetization of users and an indication of things to come in Big Tech. Indeed, the domain of gaming represents an avant-garde of business model innovation on the internet (Joseph, 2021; Nieborg, 2021), and key actors in Big Tech are taking similar directions towards microtransactions, microfinance, and virtual commerce, possibly due to the increasing regulation of advertising and the associated collection of personal data. Manzerolle et al, for instance, point to the growing integration of transactional affordances on social media platforms (Manzerolle and Wiseman, 2016; Manzerolle and Daubs, 2021), and YouTube is moving from an attention economy to an engagement economy integrating commerce directly into its interface (Ørmen and Gregersen, 2022). Meta CEO Mark Zuckerberg has taken inspiration from the revenue models of *Minecraft*, *Roblox* and *Fortnite* and hints that Meta 'would copy that strategy to make money in its own metaverse, taking a slice of every transaction' (Kovach,

2021). In this way, the intense experimentation with virtual economies and markets in the domain of gaming and the Steam platform's position at the forefront of these activities makes it a critical case of future business models beyond advertising.

Steam was introduced by Valve Corporation at the Game Developers Conference in 2003, and since around 2010, it has been the dominant platform in the field of PC gaming. In the beginning, it primarily served as a download client for Valve's own game titles, but the press release indicates that the platform was already, at the launch, envisioned as a 'multi-sided market' (Evans and Schmalensee, 2016) offering gamers as well as game publishers a range of functionalities, and by 2005, Valve started contracting with third-party publishers. Steam differs in a range of ways from other gaming platforms due to its status as a social medium, and from other social media in its business model. As concerns the differences between Steam and other game platforms, Steam's continuous development involves the addition of a range of features turning it into what Werning defines as a 'de facto social network' (Werning, 2019). That is, Steam displays a range of social affordances at the platform level, and an important aspect of its governance is the continuous nurturing and harnessing of the player communities emerging on it. The 'Steam community' features introduced in 2007 enable players to socialize and communicate outside their games in a range of ways, and since 2012, publishers on the platform have been able to create community features in relation to specific game titles. To many small publishers, this possibility of getting in direct contact with their audience is one of Steam's key attractions. Moreover, the community events organized on the Steam platform, such as seasonal sales, awards, and tournaments (Werning, 2019), play a key role in the continuous maintenance of the Steam community, the platform's primary asset. Some of Steam's primary competitors have made attempts to follow this example. For instance, Epic has organized its own tournament as part of its platform strategy. Yet, their emphases are still on game store and multiplayer features, and they do not offer the same range of options for interacting and connecting beyond individual game titles that Steam does. In this way, Werning argues, Steam has developed into a de facto social network (Werning, 2019), and its dedicated and loyal communities are part of its key business offers.

However, Valve's way of monetizing this social network in and beyond the game titles offered on the platform differs considerably from other social media platforms. Advertising is directly rejected as a business model on Steam: 'Steam does not support paid ads or referral/affiliate revenue from showing ads to other games and/or products or services. If your game's revenue relies on advertising on other platforms, you will need to find a new model to ship on Steam'.[3] Instead, Valve pushes its microtransaction system as a key alternative:

Steam places no restrictions on what you sell or how you sell it nor does it preclude the use of whatever other mechanisms your game has for selling items. Its purpose is to bring a common payment experience that user's (sic) are familiar with from the Steam platform into your game and allow them to easily spend their Steam wallet value on your products.[4]

This makes Steam a very interesting case for exploring platform business models beyond advertising. The advertising business model has been so dominant in digital platforms that advertisers are sometimes defined as platform constituencies (Gillespie, 2010) and advertisements are sometimes directly included as key aspects of platform logics (Burgess, 2021); yet, Valve takes an entirely different approach to its business by way of its 'tangled market'.

The Steam platform features a tangled market, that is, a set of interconnected and mutually dependent market contexts (see Figure 1.1). Of these the multi-sided market of the game store is the historically first and very likely still the most profitable one. In this market, publishers offer games and downloadable content (DLC) to players at a fixed price in accordance with the principles of classic retail. In addition to this, the microtransaction system is pushed at a range of levels on the platform. As the former citation indicates, Valve strongly encourages game publishers to make use of this feature, offering in-game purchases and supplementing the fixed-priced, single-payment structure of the game store with different forms of continuous upselling in the games or in 'item stores' at the level of the platform. In all these cases, game publishers act as sellers, players act as buyers, and Steam earns a share of every transaction taking place. However, Valve has also integrated its microtransaction system into contexts of the platform, including the Steam community market and community workshop, key components of the aforementioned Steam community. The Steam community market can be defined as a 'secondary market' (Lehdonvirta and Castronova, 2014) where players simultaneously participate as sellers and buyers; however, they are only allowed to exchange items obtained in games on the Steam platform. Players cannot resell entire game titles or items of their own creation; they can exchange items obtained from Steam-based games directly between their Steam inventories or list items in the Steam community market in cases where game publishers have chosen to mark these items as either 'tradable' or 'marketable', or both. Direct exchange of items between inventories is effectively a form of 'barter' and does not involve any money or alternative units of account. Once items are listed in the Steam community market, though, their fluctuating prices are specified in local currency, and Valve earns a share of every transaction taking place. Moreover, in addition to the trading of items obtained in games, players may give away their own creations for free in the Steam community workshop or they may sell them, depending on how the specific publisher has chosen to utilize the workshop features made available by the Steam platform. In the case of the latter, Valve will earn a share as well. In this way, Steam offers actors on the platform a range of strategic choices and ways of making economic transactions. Through these features, the platform shapes market interactions (Srnicek, 2017) and defines the rules of transaction (Fligstein 1996, 2001) defining who is able to sell what to whom, earning a share of every transaction taking place, as illustrated here.

As I will return to in Chapter 7, Valve's own flagship game titles make use of this framework in ways that differ considerably from other actors on the platform, addressing users simultaneously as consumers, traders, and creators in different contexts of its tangled market. In this way, Valve employs a different business strategy to the predominantly advertisement-driven digital media platforms, and a more complex market context than those of comparable market platforms such as the App Store and Google Play. The aim of this book is to explore this tangled market systematically

Figure 1.1: Steam's tangled markets

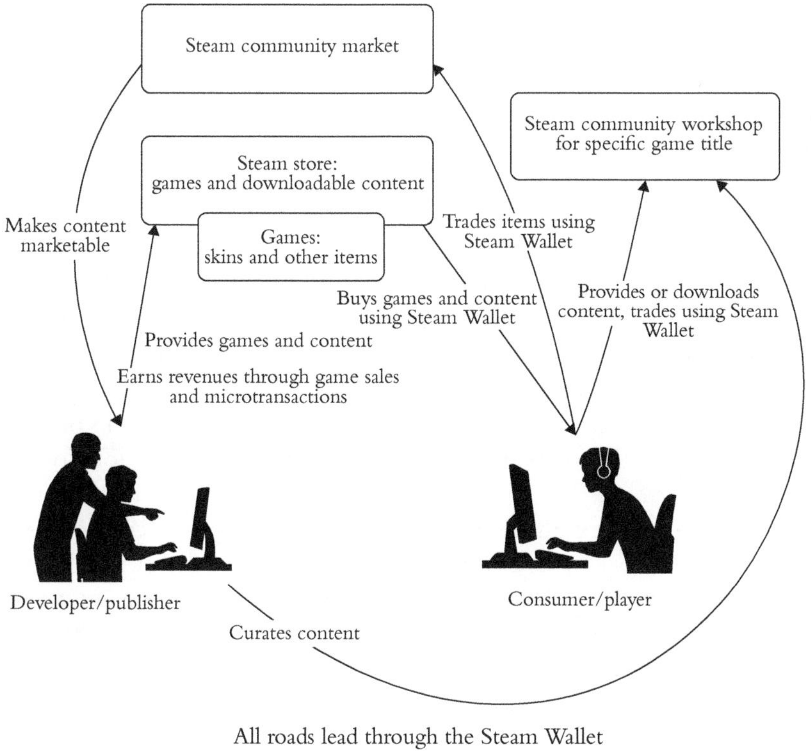

All roads lead through the Steam Wallet

and empirically, and to do this, I will apply an analytical framework based on insights from platform studies, game studies, the economic sociology of markets, affective economies, and the Marxist theory of commodification. In the following sections, I will explain this framework in more detail, addressing firstly how *platforms* have evolved in the *domain of gaming*, how *business models* have evolved along these lines, and the specific role of *player-driven economies* in these models. As an extension of this, I will introduce key concepts from the economic sociology of markets, including the *embeddedness of economic action* and *markets as fields* populated by actors typically positioned as *incumbents* and *challengers* and maintaining a given *market order*. This analytical framework will be used to explain how the reorganization of gaming communities as market interactions serve to transform affective value into market value (Chapter 5), and how different actors in the game market participate in Steam's platform economy as an extension of their different positions in the wider game market order (Chapter 7). Finally, I will address how players are simultaneously positioned as consumers, creators, and traders, and how this challenges current notions of *user commodification* on digital media platforms (Chapter 9).

Platforms in the domain of digital games

The cultural domain of digital games lends itself well to a discussion of platformization and platform economies because digital games were 'platformized' (Poell et al, 2019) from the beginning. The first digital games ran on university mainframe computers in the 1960s and their commercialized descendants found their way into malls and burger bars on so-called arcade machines and into private homes on game consoles and microcomputers in the 1970s. Throughout the 1980s and 1990s and well into the 2000s, the two latter platforms made up the key components of a two-tiered market order, where the field of console games was dominated by a small number of console owners and large publishers and the field of PC games covered a broader range of small, middle-sized, and large market actors (Kerr, 2017). This can be somewhat attributed to the technological features of the platforms in question, that is, the proprietary systems of game consoles with tightly coupled hardware and software, and the more loosely coupled platforms of PC games, produced and sold by a broader range of market actors and with different proprietary and open access software. Yet, it makes little sense to talk of these platforms without considering the ownership structures and wider market orders of which they are a part. As I will get back to in a moment, the market order of console and PC games during these early decades is an example of what Fligstein (2001) identifies as a 'stable market', where a small number of incumbents control the market and act strategically to keep challengers out. In the digital game market of the 1980s and the 1990s, owners of dominant game consoles held the position of incumbents vis-à-vis small and middle-sized actors who operated primarily in the field of PC games. During the last decade, this market order has been disrupted by new types of 'platform actors', that is, the Google, Apple, Facebook, Amazon, and Microsoft (GAFAM) (Van Dijck, 2013) industries and their Chinese counterparts, that have diversified into the domain of digital gaming. This development has brought about new genres of gaming, a 'casual revolution' (Juul, 2010) of simple games played on mobile devices, and new types of business models in the form of free-to-play games with an emphasis on advertising (Nieborg, 2016) as an alternative to the predominant publishing logic (Miège, 1987; Kerr, 2021) of traditional game platforms. Moreover, it has changed the market order of digital games so that the largest actors in the contemporary game market are now companies from outside the previous market order, who have diversified into this field (Kerr, 2021).

However, this development has also changed the very concept of *platform*. The game consoles of the 1990s fit somewhat into an early platform studies notion of 'computational or computing systems that allow developers to work creatively on them' (Bogost and Montfort, 2009: 4) and platform-driven development (Halman et al, 2003), with their emphasis on hardware and software features, and how other market actors are invited to utilize these features. However, the power held by the GAFAM industries (Van Dijck, 2013) and their Chinese counterparts is not just about controlling a computational system. Indeed, the 'platformization' of cultural and societal domains (Van Dijck et al, 2018; Poell et al, 2019) and the rise of 'infrastructural platforms' (Van Dijck et al, 2018) due to 'the scale, indispensability, and level of use typically achieved previously by infrastructures' (Plantin and Punathambekar, 2019: 169) are just as much about their characteristics as market actors and economic entities, that is, the massive financial power held by the platform owners, and how this enables them to establish and maintain market monopolies, enforce industry standards, and reorganize society in the process (Van Dijck et al, 2018; Plantin and Punathambekar, 2019). At some point in this development, the specific characteristics of platforms as 'programmable architectures' (Van Dijck, 2018) lose explanatory power, and alternative perspectives such as market position, ownership structures, and financialization become important. In Chapter 2, I will trace this changing notion of platforms as it can be identified in the domain of gaming. I will argue that it makes more sense to address these entities as 'platform configurations', in which the platform defined as a computational system represents one component with varying significance. Indeed, it is worth asking whether the 'platform power' of certain companies should be attributed to the platform prefix or whether we are talking about plain financial power. In the chapter, I will demonstrate how the different segments of the game industry, as identified by Aphra Kerr, can be meaningfully described as 'platform configurations' leading to different types of platform logics, from the strongly controlled market of console games and the somewhat more open market of PC games to the vast storefronts of Google, Apple, and Tencent.

Business models of game platforms

The domain of digital games also provides an alternative perspective on platform business models beyond that of advertising. Advertising is prevalent in contemporary platform economies, including those of gaming platforms, and for the same reason, it holds a key role in academic studies of platforms and platform economies. For instance, in his pivotal work on the politics of platforms, Tarleton Gillespie (Gillespie, 2010: 348) defines advertising as one of the constituencies of platforms to which platform owners must present its service. Similarly, Jean Burgess, in her introduction to platform studies (Burgess, 2021), includes advertising as a key aspect of the 'platform logics' that frame the production of cultural content on platforms:

> Platform logics shape what counts as value (for example, in the form of audience attention or engagement) and how that value is measured (whether by clicks, subscriptions, watch time, or a combination of these). Platforms convert those measurements into semiautomated decisions about which content is pushed to audiences and the extent to which that content can attract advertising revenue. (2021: 23)

Indeed, the notions of surveillance and 'surveillance capitalism' (Zuboff, 2015, 2019) somewhat presupposes the business model of advertising, since a key incentive for the commercial surveillance of users in the first place is that their attention can be segmented and sold to advertisers. In this way, advertising is a somewhat implicit backdrop to key works in critical platform studies. As I have already pointed out, there are good reasons for this emphasis since advertising is certainly a dominant business model in digital platform economies and in the media industries historically. Still, it is not the only one possible, and the varying business models of digital games and the platforms on which they are played allow for a further elaboration and discussion of this aspect of platforms. The production logic (Miège, 1987) of the early market of console and PC games was based on publication (Kerr, 2021) with a business emphasis on retail rather than advertising (Kerr, 2017). This emphasis somewhat persists in their contemporary incarnations, with the primary difference being that distribution and retail are increasingly integrated into the platforms' digital storefronts, with the decline of physical retail as a result. Indeed, the move to online distribution observed by Kerr (2017) has transformed traditional game platform owners into online retailers. In comparison, the new platform actors' entrance into this market has introduced advertising as an alternative business model in gaming, with implications for the development and circulation of games at a number of levels. David Nieborg (2015) demonstrates how the business models of Facebook and Apple shape the features of the casual game title *Candy Crush Saga* as a 'connective commodity' reflecting the specific business interests of the platforms on which it runs through their emphasis on 'product commodities', 'prosumer commodities', and 'player commodities'. The rise of the 'player commodity' (Nieborg, 2016) in gaming is comparable to that of the 'audience commodity' (Smythe, 1981) in commercial media more generally, and in this way, the traditional publishing and retail logic of core console and PC games is complemented with the advertising logic of Facebook and Apple in the case of casual games running on touchscreen devices.

However, this new domain of games also involves an alternative business model of microtransactions, that is, continuous opt-in payments as an alternative to the emphasis on the initial point-of-sale characteristic of traditional retail. In this business model, emphasis is to a lesser degree on user data and user attention, and to a larger degree on users' willingness to continuously pay small (or large) amounts of money as part of their gaming activity. Of course, user data still plays a role in identifying those users who are more willing to pay and may also have value in the secondary market of data harvesters or as an offset of marketing costs, but it does not represent a key component of the business model as it does in advertising. The Epic/Apple lawsuit over microtransaction policies[5] indicates the relative importance of this business model. This dispute concerns whether Epic is obligated to use the App Store's microtransaction system when the massively popular game title *Fortnite* is accessed from this platform, or whether Epic can use its own in-game microtransaction system. Ultimately, this is about whether Apple can take a 30 per cent share of every microtransaction made by players accessing *Fortnite* from the App Store. Though it is probably not a majority of *Fortnite* users accessing the game in this way, it is still a considerable amount of money given that microtransactions pushed forward by sales of virtual items form a key component of *Fortnite*'s business model (Thorhauge and Nielsen, 2021). This is very likely the reason why Epic has launched its own platform as a direct challenge to Steam's dominant position in the domain of PC gaming.

The platforms' share of microtransactions has somewhat passed beneath the radar of inquiries into user monetization on digital platforms, as this has been an issue between platform and publisher. Yet, in the case of business models based on economic transactions like the ones we find on gaming and on 'lean platforms' (Srnicek, 2017) such as Airbnb and Uber, it is directly tied to users' economic interaction. These business models are not really part of the 'attention economy' associated with digital media platform economies but rather built on attracting market actors such as game publishers or landlords, and maximizing economic transactions on the platforms, by setting the rules of market interactions (2017: 47). The notions of 'multi-sided markets' or 'matchmakers' (Evans and Schmalensee, 2016) are sometimes invoked to address this aspect of platform markets, and in Chapter 3, I will discuss in more detail how this has been applied to platforms. As I will get back to in a moment, the notion of 'multi-sided markets' builds on a classic economic notion of markets, while the economic-sociological approach I will suggest in this book allows for a more detailed analysis of the market contexts and market actors on the Steam platform.

The role of player-driven economies

The domains of digital games in general and online multiplayer games in particular provide a distinctive perspective on the way market interactions are strategically shaped by platform owners to maximize economic transactions and generate profit. This is due to the inherently economic nature of many types of gameplay sometimes involving player-driven economies. Player-driven economies popularly refer to a group of massive multiplayer online games that build on players' active gathering and trading of resources in the game (for example, Eve Online and RuneScape), and have also been theorized as 'virtual economies' by Eduard Castronova (Castronova, 2006). In the terminology of Lehdonvirta and Castronova (2014: 85), these games feature 'unregulated markets' where players simultaneously participate as buyers and sellers generating emergent and complex virtual economies and price formations. This economic aspect of gameplay is not unique to digital games, of course. Classic game titles like Monopoly and Risk also involve the strategic acquisition and management of finite resources no matter if these resources are labelled as money, tokens, or military units. And once communities of gamers or fans emerge in relation to particular game titles and fictional universes, these game economies blend with markets in ways that depend equally on the specific design of the game or the fictional universe in question and the way inventive economic actors transform this into economic practices beyond the game. A case in point is the avid trading communities arising in relation to *Magic: The Gathering* cards in the 1990s and 2000s, which took a substantial step up once they moved online. As trading was no longer confined to local contexts and buyers and sellers could be found anywhere, this economy grew immensely. Indeed, the contemporary secondary market of *Magic: The Gathering* trading cards has reached a volume that turns these cards into potentially viable investment assets in a wider financial perspective (Weber, 2021).

As early as 2001, Castronova (2001) published an economic report on the player-driven economy emerging in relation to the online multiplayer game *Everquest*, complete with BNP per capita, average income, and exchange rate of the in-game currency as compared to a range of conventional state-issued currencies. At that particular time in history, the currency of *Everquest* had higher exchange rates than the Japanese yen and the Italian lira. In a later publication, Castronova defines these game economies as 'synthetic worlds' and emphasizes the blurred boundaries between these and surrounding economies (Castronova, 2006). Indeed, Castronova and Lehdonvirta have written an entire guide to the design of virtual economies as key aspects of the design of game in general (2014). While their emphasis is on the way insights from classic economy can inform the design of compelling gameplays in digital games, they also include a section on the achievements of virtual economies with regard to the monetization of users. One great achievement of the sale of virtual goods, they point out, is that it allows for 'dynamic pricing', that is, price discrimination by way of costumer self-selection allowing the game publisher to earn the maximum from every costumer segment. This is opposed to flat-rate payment, which only addresses the acceptable price level of particular customer segments, while keeping out those who are willing to pay less and earning suboptimally from those who are willing to pay more (2014: 14–15). While they address the game world as general economic systems, they also analyse more specifically the design and maintenance of markets. In this way, player-driven economies can, on one hand, be defined as part of the fun, a gameplay feature that increases the complexity of in-game economies in interesting ways and adds to the gaming experience and perhaps even generates an economic 'metagame' within the game, while, on the other hand, they are at the core of the 'free lunch' business model of online gaming.

Everquest runs on its own online client, and it is an open question whether this game economy should be labelled a platform economy or not. I will explore this in more detail in Chapter 2; however, my key point is that the intersection between player-driven economies and markets represents a lucrative spot for a range of business strategies, such as maximizing demand for certain in-game items, taxing economic transactions, and exploiting different exchange rates between in-game and conventional currencies, and that this intersection represents an alternative perspective on platform business models to that of advertising. In my analysis of Steam's tangled markets in Chapters 5 to 8, I will demonstrate how the strategic shaping of player-driven economies represents an important business interest at the platform level from a range of perspectives. I will show how the platforms' development over time indicates an increasing emphasis on maximizing economic transactions on the platform (Chapter 5), how this is reflected in the current platform features (Chapter 6), how different economic actors on the platform, including the platform owner itself, transform these affordances into different business strategies (Chapter 7), and how these economies are integrated into wider economic practices on the internet in ways that serve the economic interests of the platform owner (Chapter 8). To conduct this analysis, I will apply key concepts from the field of economic sociology.

An economic–sociological approach to markets

The notion of markets is not new to platform studies or to game studies. As I pointed out earlier in this introduction, the notion of multi-sided markets is often invoked to explain the market features of platforms. For instance, Van Dijck et al (2018) note that 'economic exchange enabled by platforms … takes place in a structure best understood as multi-sided markets' (Van Dijck et al, 2018: 37–8). Moreover, Srnicek (2017) points out that 'the rules of product and service development as well as marketplace interactions are set by the platform owner' (Srnicek, 2017: 47). It is not entirely clear, though, if multi-sided markets are considered a defining part or just a potential feature of digital platforms, or if all interactions on digital platforms should be considered marketplace interactions. As I have also touched upon, game economies and markets have received considerable attention in the field of game studies, such as Castronovas' work on game economies and Lehdonvirta and Castronovas' introduction to the analysis and design of virtual economies. Common to the emphasis on multi-sided markets in platform studies and the design of game economies in game studies is that they both apply a classic economic perspective to economies and markets, applying a range of standard terms from this field such as supply and demand, market forms, and exchange mechanisms. However, the notion of markets is more or less taken for granted in the field of classic economics and is seldom directly defined.

Most popular accounts apply a range of adjectives such as free, competitive, and fully informed, yet what constitutes a market in itself is not defined. Obviously, classic economists do occupy themselves with markets in a range of ways that allows for an inferred definition. For instance, markets have been approached as distinctive forms of economic organization that differ from firms and hierarches (Williamson, 1973). Moreover, a large area of classic economic research concerns price formations in markets, turning the price mechanism into a primary and perhaps definitory feature of markets from a classic economic perspective. In comparing the notion of markets in classic economy and illegal markets, for instance, Murjii states that while the market 'refers to the conditions of supply and demand in economics, in criminology it refers largely to a realm of illegal behaviors and transactions' (Murji, 2007: 782). In this book, I will apply an economic-sociological perspective on markets for a range of reasons. An economic-sociological perspective allows me to address more specifically the relationship between social interaction and economic interaction and the overlaps between the two in a platform-economic perspective. Moreover, an economic-sociological perspective allows me to address platform owners as well as the different complementors (Van Dijck et al, 2018) operating on these platforms as empirical market actors, positioned in specific and historically contingent fields or market orders. For this purpose, I will engage two key perspectives from the field of economic sociology: the concept of embeddedness, as this appears in Polanyi's historical account of market society (Polanyi, 1944), and in later network-analytical approaches (Granovetter, 1985). Moreover, I will apply Fligstein's notion of markets as fields populated by various market actors acting strategically to challenge or maintain a certain order (Fligstein, 1996, 2001).

Polanyi's historical account of market society (Polanyi, 1944) concerns the process through which economic action is institutionally separated from other types of action. He points out that trade existed in a range of forms before the emergence of the modern market institution, yet, in these contexts, trade was *embedded* into the social structures in which it took place. For instance, local trade was a ritual celebration and reproduction of local communities and served the purposes of these rather than its own ends. According to Polanyi, the emergence of the modern market institution is closely associated with the historical emergence of the national state and the Industrial Revolution and implied the institutional separation of economic action from the rest of society to a point where economic action increasingly dictates the social rather than the other way around: 'instead of the economy being embedded in social relations, social relations are embedded in the economy' (1944: 60). Polanyi's concept has later been taken up and somewhat transformed by the new economic sociology, where it points to the fact that economic actors are always *embedded* into social networks that shape their economic actions. This understanding of the concept was introduced by Granovetter along a network-analytical approach to social embeddedness, emphasizing economic actors' position in social networks as a key perspective on the knowledge they are able to obtain and the economic actors they are able to connect with (Granovetter, 1985). This approach to embeddedness differs considerably from Polanyi's; indeed, Greta Krippner defines it as an inversion of the original concept (Krippner, 2001). A somewhat kinder interpretation could be that Polanyi addresses the institutional level, while Granovetter addresses the level of social networks. In the first case, the focus is on the separation of the economic and the social at the level of institutions; in the second, the focus is on the intersection between the economic and the social at the level of social networks.

Nevertheless, both perspectives are relevant for my analysis of the way the Steam platform features strategically define and shape market interactions. Thus, I will argue that Steam's value extraction mechanism can be defined as a process of 'disembedment' in which players' economic actions are detached from the player-driven economies of which they are a part and reorganized as market interactions. A key example is the controversy arising in relation to the introduction of 'paid mods' in the Steam community workshop (Joseph, 2018). The steam community workshop was introduced as a service to the 'modding communities' that have turned the modification of digital games into a hobby and are often associated with a range of somewhat ambiguous non-industry values (Banks, 2013). That is, the modifications are (at least by some) considered common goods created for the sake of the community, and thus, it spawned a great deal of controversy when Valve introduced the options of selling and buying mods in the Steam community workshop, in practice by integrating the platform's microtransaction system with this part of the platform. With reference to Harvey's concept of 'accumulation by dispossession', Daniel Joseph defines this as 'digital dispossession', that is, 'the modders were momentarily "dispossessed" of their labor by the paid mods program' (Joseph, 2018: 696). He continues to argue that while this might be the immediate interpretation of some of the implied actors, the introduction of paid mods also reveals the nature of modding as unpaid labour as such. In applying Polanyi's concept of embeddedness, I argue that this value extraction mechanism can, at a more general level, be defined as a 'dispossession by disembedment' that reaches far beyond the context of the Steam community workshop. Indeed, the monetization of player-driven economies can, at a general level, be described as a transformation of shared values in gaming communities into market value through the reorganization of players' economic interactions into market interactions. In Chapter 5, I will map the Steam platform's development of features over time in order to demonstrate how the continuous addition and discontinuation of features reflect an increasing business emphasis on player communities and various ways of monetizing these. In Chapter 6, I will analyse in more detail how the steam platform in its contemporary form enables a range of contexts for economic exchange, and in Chapter 7, I will map how different actors on the platform transform these spaces into business strategies. Finally, in Chapter 8, I will show how entrepreneurs operating on third-party websites extend economic practices beyond the platform in ways that contribute to the overall platform economy.

As concerns Fligstein's notion of markets as fields (Fligstein, 1996, 2001), I will use this approach to markets to address how different actors, including Valve itself, transform these affordances into business strategies, and what this can tell us about the market order on and beyond the Steam platform. As a theory of markets, Fligstein breaks with perhaps the most crucial aspect of the classic economic approach to markets, that is, that markets are inherently competitive. Quite oppositely, Fligstein argues, strategic interaction in markets is often aimed at mitigating the detrimental effects of competition.

Moreover, he emphasizes the key role of the state in creating and maintaining markets through various types of regulation. Thus, Fligstein defines the basic components of market institutions as property rights, governance structures, laws, institutional practices, conceptions of control, and rules of exchange (Fligstein, 1996: 658). He also distinguishes between incumbents and challengers as different types of economic actors in the market field who act strategically to maintain or challenge a given market order. As an extension of this train of thought, a stable market is characterized by the dominance of a few established incumbents who act strategically to keep challengers out. In emerging markets, this order is still to be established, as this is where markets are most likely to feature the competition idealized by classic economists. In markets in crisis, a disturbance typically from nearby markets has shaken the order maintained by existing incumbents, and new actors enter the order. As appears from this very short summary, Fligstein's notion of markets as fields describes very well how the order of the digital game market was organized around a few console owners and large publishers in the 1980s and 1990s who acted strategically to keep challengers out, and how this market order was disrupted by the nearby market of tech in the 2000s and 2010s, leading to a new market order dominated by a new kind of platform actor (Kerr, 2017). Moreover, this 'portrait' of the contemporary game markets can be used to contextualize the role of Steam within the wider game market, and to analyse the significance of specific economic actors' absence or presence on the Steam platform as a 'local market order'. In Chapter 8, I will address how different market actors are positioned in the Steam market order, including how their varying ways of leveraging the Steam platform features reflect their position in the Steam store, their position within the wider market order, and their specific role in the Steam platform economy.

Commodification of economic action?

When player-driven economies become key components of platform business models and intensified economic transactions become a key business strategy, the economic actions of individual platform users become the key value-generating activities on the platform. This raises some fundamental questions about the ways users are monetized on these types of platforms and whether these scenarios can be interpreted within the existing analytical frameworks of user commodification (Manzerolle, 2010; Nieborg, 2015) and user labour (Terranova, 2000; Fuchs, 2014) on digital platforms. That economic action can take the form of labour is obvious. For instance, banks, hedge funds, and other actors in the financial markets employ brokers who trade currencies and securities as part of their day job. Depending on the form of renumeration, they earn a salary for doing so, or they earn a share of the profits they generate. In the case of Steam, players are not employees and do not earn a salary from the platform, and the profits generated from their economic actions are considered to be their own. In practice, Steam credits and items remain tied to the platform and can only be converted into conventional currencies if the user involves one of the third-party websites who offer this service (see Joseph, 2021; Thorhauge, forthcoming). Moreover, Steam does not represent an actor in a financial market; it constitutes *the* entire market or context of economic exchange in which players conduct their economic action. Nevertheless, their economic action in the different contexts of economic exchange offered on the platform generates value for the platform owner, either through direct shares of the transactions taking place or from the entire economy expanding as a consequence of players' economic action.

Existing approaches to user commodification and labour on digital media platforms typically focus on the creation and consumption of content (Fuchs, 2014), and the notions of audience, prosumer, and player commodities (Manzerolle, 2010; Fuchs, 2014; Nieborg 2015, 2016) typically place their emphasis on advertising as the central business model. In his seminal work on the audience commodity (1981), Smythe reframes the audience itself as the true product of commercial media, that is, the primary business of commercial media is not to deliver content to audiences but to deliver audiences to advertisers. As an extension of this, Smythe introduces the notion of 'audience work' as a denominator of the behaviour audiences must conform to in this business model. The notion of audience work has led to some dispute in the Marxist tradition of which Smythe is a part; however, it does find resonance in more recent work on immaterial labour in the context of the internet (Terranova, 2000), and the notion of the audience commodity has gained renewed interest as a perspective on the ways users are commodified and monetized on digital platforms more recently. The concept has been somewhat customized for this purpose and a range of extended definitions has been introduced, such as the player commodity (Nieborg, 2016), the prosumer commodity (Fuchs, 2011), and the mobile prosumer commodity (Manzerolle, 2010). Yet, common to these definitions is that they all (like Smythe) assume advertising to be the primary commercial framework. For this reason, the position of the consumer or potential buyer of products in the market remains the primary point of departure. For instance, Fuchs point out that 'One accumulation strategy is to give them free access to services and platforms, let them produce content, and to accumulate a large number of prosumers that are sold as a commodity to third-party advertisers' (Fuchs, 2011: 153). However, when players perform various sorts of economic action in player-driven economies and in market contexts, they are simultaneously micro-capitalists within the virtual or real economies of the platform in question, and 'labourers' in the sense that their economic action generates value for the platform owner, either directly through a share of transactions or indirectly by adding to the growth of the economy and hence the capital that can be invested elsewhere. Accordingly, a closer examination of the way player-driven economies are monetized on digital platforms also calls for a reconsideration of the way economic action fits into existing frameworks of user commodification and labour on platforms.

In Chapter 5, I will describe and discuss the reorganization or 'disembedding' of player-driven economies into market interactions as a way of transforming the affective value generated in gaming communities into actual market value that can be taxed, reinvested, and leveraged for other purposes. Within this framework, players' participation in game economies and the value they attach to the game world and its content represents a first important step towards monetizing gameplay. While game items may gain additional value due to other factors once integrated into the market, what makes them worth trading in the first instance is the value attached to them within gaming communities. It is this value that is transformed into market value by introducing the option of direct economic transactions in a range of contexts on the platform. In Chapter 5, I will analyse in more detail how this business approach is reflected in the continuous feature changes on the Steam platform, including the integration of 'transactional affordances' (Manzerolle and Wiseman, 2016; Manzerolle and Daubs, 2021) into a range of contexts. In my concluding chapter, I will return to this discussion and suggest that Steam's tangled market calls for a reconsideration of the notion of user commodification. Indeed, all steps from the creation and consumption of content to the trading of virtual goods can potentially be commodified within contemporary platform business models, from the commodification of user-generated content over the strategic reorganization of player-driven economies to the commodification of users themselves.

Reading guide

The primary contributions of this book include a systematic description of the Steam platform business model, which differs in significant ways from others in the domain of digital media platforms. Moreover, I suggest a theoretical framework for addressing in more detail digital platforms' market features based on economic-sociological theories of markets, and I illustrate how this can be used for interrogating market platforms systematically and critically at a more general level. Finally, I suggest an analytical expansion of the concept of user commodification that includes economic action on platforms. The chapters are organized in the following way:

- In Chapter 2, I interrogate critically the notion of platforms and how this phenomenon has developed historically in the domain of digital games. I suggest the notion of platform configuration as a more accurate expression of what we're looking at. Moreover, I explain how the business models of digital games have changed as an extension of this historical development.
- In Chapter 3, I take a closer look at the market component of digital platforms, including how this aspect has been addressed from the perspective of platform studies and how key concepts from the economic sociology of markets may elaborate it. I suggest the notion of 'tangled market' as a way of understanding the range of interconnected and mutually dependent market contexts on and beyond the Steam platform and the business logic this involves.
- In Chapter 4, I provide a little more historical context to Valve Corporation and the Steam platform as the primary case of this book. Moreover, I explain the relationship between the individual chapters of the analysis and the methods and data that undergird them.
- In Chapter 5, I map the Steam platform's feature changes over time, including the strategic expansion of the scope of economic transactions on the platform as an indication of Valve's business emphases beyond the contexts of the game store. I suggest that one key value extraction mechanism on the Steam platform is the conversion of affective value into market value through the strategic reorganization of player interactions as market interactions.
- In Chapter 6, I analyse how these continuous feature changes are expressed in Steam's current platform features, with an emphasis on the way economic transactions are enabled and shaped across a range of contexts of the platform. I draw a general map of Steam's tangled markets and point out the Steam Wallet and the microtransaction system as those key features that define Steam's business model.
- In Chapter 7, I map how different types of market actors transform these affordances into business strategies. As a platform, Steam depends on various entrepreneurs to transform its affordances into concrete economic interactions; however, these actors are also part of a more general market order in which Valve Corporation holds a certain position. I argue that the presence and absence of specific market actors on the Steam platform and the business strategies they employ are simultaneously an expression of the designed affordances offered by Steam as well the wider market order of which it is a part.
- In Chapter 8, I broaden the perspective to the third-party trading and gambling that exist independently of the Steam platform, yet depend on Steam to complete their transactions. Though Steam does not earn a direct share of these transactions, I argue that they indirectly represent an

economic advantage to Valve, as they help raise the demand for 'skins' and thus grow the entire Steam platform economy. Moreover, I argue that the Steam platform and these websites in combination can be interpreted as a 'monetary network' connecting the Steam platform economy to wider economic practices on the internet and potentially transforming the platform into an instrument of payment beyond its own game economies.

• In the ninth and concluding chapter, I address the wider implications of this platform business model in terms of the way users are monetized and commodified. I argue that the user is simultaneously addressed as consumer, producer, and market actor on the Steam platform and that all acts of production, consumption, and economic exchange are in this way commodified. This adds an important new dimension to the audience commodity in its various forms and raises new questions about the regulation of digital platforms and platform markets. I conclude that the Steam platform business model is not sufficiently addressed in current legal frameworks with their emphasis on personal data, and that digital platforms as an extension of Steam's business model should also be regulated as markets and financial technologies.

I expect this book to be relevant to academics in the fields of platform studies, game studies, and sociology, including economic sociology and the sociology of consumption. People in platform studies might take most interest in Chapter 2 about the way game platforms resemble and differ from other platforms. People in game studies may want to skip the theoretical framework entirely and focus on my analysis of the Steam platform in Chapters 5 to 8. People in economic sociology may take primary interest in the way I interpret key texts within their field in Chapter 4, and how this is put to use in Chapters 5, 7, and 8. People in the sociology of consumption might take most interest in the concluding chapter, where I reconsider the relationship between production and consumption as seen from the perspective of player-driven economies. Finally, graduate and undergraduate students within any of these fields may want to stick to this introduction and get their assignments done in time!

2

Platform Configurations in Gaming

In this chapter, I will address the way platforms have developed in the field of digital gaming and use this historical backdrop for interrogating critically the notion of platforms. The historical development of gaming platforms can help us to question what should indeed be attributed to the platform as a computational system and what should rather be explained by the platform owner's financial status and position within the wider market context. Traditional game consoles are, in practice, proprietary innovation platforms, in Gawer's (2011) and Cusumano's (2010) sense, a set of development and publishing tools and a key contact point to the gaming audience made available to complementors on certain conditions. As developer and publisher, you must contract with the platform owner to get your game title on the console, and as a gamer, you must purchase the console to be able to play your games. In this way, the gaming consoles of the 1980s and 1990s effectively inserted themselves between game publishers and the gaming audience in the same manner as contemporary platforms are said to do, and their specific design and forms of governance indicate a certain market order, that is, a certain field of incumbents and challengers (see Chapter 3). Their power is that of the traditional book publisher owning the key to a particular version of the book format, which happens to be the market standard. These platforms were a key principle in the consumer game market from the 1980s onwards, and the key distinction of the 1990s game market was not drawn between platformized and non-platformized cultural production (Nieborg and Poell, 2018) but rather between proprietary platforms such as PlayStation and open platforms such as the PC. Accordingly, the 2010s market did not mark a new era of platformization but rather the introduction of a new type of platform and a new integration of platforms and markets.

As Aphra Kerr observes, one key trend in the game market during the past decade has been a further concentration of ownership and market domination by an even smaller number of actors, such as Microsoft, Apple, Tencent, and Google (Kerr, 2017). These are the sorts of companies that we have become used to referring to as 'platforms', that is, Big Tech companies that have 'expanded diagonally' (Doyle, 2013) into the field of gaming and turned the game market into a part of their monopolization and cross-subsidization strategies (Srnicek, 2017). The development described by Kerr is effectively an integration of the game market into the more general market order shaped by the GAFAM industries (Van Dijck, 2013) and their Chinese counterparts. This development also changes the notion of platforms from that of proprietary systems offering a set of development and publishing tools to that of huge market actors or even monopolies, who use their financial power to dominate markets. Moreover, these actors gain their power in the game market from their storefronts, effectively integrating retail into their platforms. The power has changed from that of the publisher to that of the retailer. Of course, as Kerr notes, the change to online distribution and retail is a general trend in the game industry, and the owners of traditional game consoles have also been quick to integrate storefronts into their platforms. In this way, the change towards online distribution and retail has consolidated the 'platform power' of game consoles, by adding retail to its domain of control.

Microsoft, Apple, Tencent, and Google, due to their financial power, control an ever greater part of the market. What characterizes these actors, then, is not just their control over proprietary systems (though proprietary systems such as Windows and iOS certainly play a key role) but also that they are basically large enough to enforce these as industry standards (Fligstein, 2001; see Chapter 3). At some point in this development, it is worth asking what is truly platform power in the technical sense and what is just plain financial power and a reflection of platform companies' status as assets in wider financial markets (Langley and Leyshon, 2017). In this chapter, I will firstly give a very brief outline of the way platforms have developed in the field of digital games. After this, I will summarize approaches within platform research into four general themes: platforms as programmable architectures, multi-sided markets, infrastructures, and practices. Based on this, I will suggest 'platform configuration' as a more precise term, including the platform-as-programmable-architecture along with market actors, market orders, and ownership structures. I will use this approach to discuss how current segments in the game industry, as identified by Kerr (2017), can be analysed as prototypical examples of platform configurations and the business models they involve.

Arcades, consoles, and digital storefronts

While the very first digital games were played on university mainframe computers in the 1960s, digital games' commercial breakthrough came in the 1970s when so-called arcade machines became a common sight in malls, burger bars, and gaming arcades. Already at this early stage of the industry, the scene was dominated by American and Japanese firms, a geographic duopoly that has characterized the game industry until relatively recently, when big Chinese platforms have joined and transformed this duopoly into an oligopoly. Contrary to later platforms, the very first arcade machines and consoles were 'hardwired', that is, they were built for specific game titles. In this way, they were introduced to the market in continuation of the pinball machines and 'one-armed bandits', which were also a common sight in public spaces at the time (Poole, 2000: 19).

However, during the same decade, digital games found their way into private homes, driven by the commercial growth of dedicated gaming consoles such as Atari and the Nintendo entertainment system, and delivering new game titles to these consoles became a major business. During this historical period, 'microcomputers' also found their way into private homes by way of the computer hobbyist movement and became another significant gaming platform representing a more open market. Sony and Nintendo were already, at this point, major players in the burgeoning industry. The industry rose at an impressive speed and had already, by 1983, experienced its first 'bubble'. However, at this point in time, the contours of the contemporary game industry were laid out with the shared dominance of American- and Japanese-owned consoles and the compound market of dedicated gaming consoles and multi-purpose home computers. While the dedicated gaming consoles were produced and distributed for the purpose of gaming only, gaming was one among many possible purposes of the newly invented private computer. Also, while consoles were proprietary systems, controlled by the platform owner and supplied with games developed by themselves and authorized developers, home computers and their operating systems were more open to potential developers and publishers. That is, while console owners controlled who could publish on their platforms with strict licensing agreements, operating systems in PCs did not involve the same degree of gatekeeping (Kerr, 2017: 130). Owners of game consoles throughout the 1990s strongly controlled who could deliver games for their platforms and deliberately limited the number of published titles (Kerr, 2017). This pattern was somewhat disrupted with the popularization of general internet access throughout the 1990s and into the beginning of the new millennium, which turned online distribution and online multiplayer gaming into a new business field. Thus, around the turn of the millennium, networked PC gaming in so-called massively multiplayer online role-playing games (MMORPGs) became a major phenomenon in the field of digital gaming. While this was obviously not an alternative to PC gaming, it granted publishers themselves an option to create and control their own clients on the internet, as an alternative or supplement to publishing on the game consoles.

Moreover, the development of smartphones and tablets throughout the first decade of the millennium brought about a 'casual revolution' (Juul, 2010), a new type of 'pick-up-and-play game' that addressed a broader audience than the traditional gamer, and soon became a major business segment, catching up with the console segment according to the industry's own numbers.[1] This business segment was closely tied to a new group of business actors entering the game market, that is, the GAFAM industries (Van Dijck, 2013) – or what we now refer to as 'platforms' – along with their Chinese counterparts. This brought about a change in the group of key actors at the top of the digital game industry, which is now dominated by Big Tech corporates. These actors did not start out in gaming, and their 'platforms' are not primarily for gaming. Their power base rests on their control of the retail through their storefronts, which are effectively key entry points to their platforms.

The platform in platforms

This very short history of platforms in the digital game industry indicates a development from arcade machines and gaming consoles to online and mobile applications controlled by large platform companies. It makes little sense to view this solely as a technological development, though, as the concept of 'platform' points to very different technological principles, and the development in terms of value chains, business models, market actors, and ownership structures is just as important as the platform itself. This development should rather be addressed as a succession of 'platform configurations', with the platform-as-computational-system representing one among several components. Before I turn to this discussion, however, I will briefly address how the concept of 'platforms' has been approached in the field of platform studies.

Platforms as programmable architectures

In their early incarnations, platforms were defined as open technological systems that invited 'complementors' to join in (Cusumano, 2010; Gawer, 2011). 'Platform thinking' was outlined as a superior competitive strategy, aimed at leveraging the network effects of the interactions it supported. The concept developed in manufacturing and was further elaborated in the field of computational systems, which may be one of the reasons for the emphasis on programmability as one important aspect of platforms (Gillespie, 2010). This understanding of platforms is echoed in later definitions, such as the 'programmable digital architecture designed to organize interactions between users' (Van Dijck et al, 2018: 9) and 'digital infrastructures that enable two or more groups to interact' (Srnicek, 2017: 43). The emphasis on programmable architectures is also prevalent in the specific branch of platform studies that has emerged in game studies represented by the MIT book series on platform studies edited by Nick Montfort and Ian Bogost, where platforms are defined as 'the hardware and software design of standardized computing systems' (2009: 2) The first book in the MIT book series on platform studies was a historical study of the Atari platform (Montfort and Bogost, 2009), and later books in the series include studies of the Nintendo entertainment systems (Altice, 2015) and the Nintendo Wii (Jones and Thiruvathukal, 2012). These studies generally deal with platforms primarily as technological systems and particular configurations of hardware and software, and, to some degree, also with the different user groups appropriating and modifying these platforms. One important aspect of platforms as programmable architectures is their API, or 'application programming interfaces', that define which data third-party developers will be able to get from or add to the platform, as well as the specific functions they will be able to make use of. This aspect of platforms has been scrutinized in detail in the field of software studies as this is one of the features that defines the degree and nature of the openness towards third-party developers and frames the flow of data to and from the platform (Helmond, 2015). In my analysis of the Steam platform in Chapters 5 and 6, I will map it as a 'programmable digital architecture' that changes over time and how it shapes economic interactions on the platform in its current form.

Platforms as multi-sided markets

Another approach to platforms in platform studies concerns their characteristics as 'multi-sided markets' (Evans and Schmalensee, 2016; Parker et al, 2016; Steinberg, 2019) that shape marketplace interactions (Srnicek, 2017) between actors and groups. Accordingly, another cluster of literature deals more specifically with the way platforms as economic spaces are configured in accordance with certain business interests, such as the location of 'profit centres' and 'loss leaders' (Rochet and Tirole, 2003). For instance, Kim and Min suggest a categorization of platforms as either suppliers (producer-oriented), tailors (consumer-oriented), or facilitators (both), focusing on where the 'value stream' of the platform starts out (Kim and Min, 2019). As I will get back to in the subsequent chapter, this business model is not specific to digital platforms; it existed decades ago, and it is not very clear if all digital platforms can be defined as multi-sided markets. Yet, it is a useful framework for understanding service platforms (Kenney and Zysman, 2020) or lean platforms (Srnicek, 2017) such as Uber and Airbnb, and it is broadly considered an aspect of platforms and platformization (Van Dijck et al, 2018).

While the notion of platforms in the field of game studies has been closely tied to Montfort and Bogost's notion of standardized computing systems, some scholars have addressed the market features of gaming platforms, such as Jöckel et al's analysis of Steam's value chain (Jöckel et al, 2008) and Werning's study of Steam's platformization strategy (Werning, 2019). Indeed, the notion of platforms as multi-sided markets goes very well with the different actors operating in the game market. The general trend towards online distribution and retail means that most dedicated gaming platforms offer different kinds of 'storefronts' that go hand in hand with the basic functionality and multiplayer services these platforms also offer. The storefront in this perspective is just another 'fixed role market' (see next chapter), where producers (game publishers) offer their goods to consumers (gamers). Indeed, the current state of the game market can to some degree be seen as a 'battle of storefronts' such as the Epic–Apple lawsuit over microtransactions mentioned in the Introduction and various companies' attempts at challenging Steam's position in the PC gaming market. In the subsequent chapter, I will address in more detail the market component of digital platforms, and in my analysis of the Steam platform in Chapters 5 to 8, I will demonstrate how it can be considered a 'tangled market', that is, a set of interconnected and mutually dependent contexts of economic exchange that enable market actors – entrepreneurs and users alike – to engage in economic interaction in accordance with specific rules of transaction (Fligstein, 1996, 2001).

Platforms as infrastructures and organizational forms

While the notion of platforms as multi-sided markets has been broadly accepted, it has also been problematized from a range of perspectives. Stark and Pais (2020) state that platforms as organizational forms differ from markets in distinctive ways. While markets contract, they argue, platforms co-opt; they acquire resources they do not own, and they manage users that are not their employees by way of algorithmic management. Peck and Philips (2020) go one step further and define platforms as 'antimarket' as an extension of Fernand Braudel's concept, that is, platforms are basically machines for the 'concentration of power and monopolization of markets' that goes against the idea of the market. This critique finds some resonance in the work of Langley and Leyshon, who point out that platforms are also financial assets in a wider quest of venture money (2017). I will return to these critiques in the subsequent chapter.

Somewhat as an extension of this focus on the monopolizing tendencies of contemporary platforms comes another cluster of research focusing on platforms as infrastructures. The notion of infrastructures is somewhat ambiguous here, as it is sometimes used synonymously with architectures (as in the previous Srnicek citation), sometimes with reference to the material foundation of digital networks (DeNardis, 2012), and sometimes in a more abstract sense as the situation where platforms reach 'the scale, indispensability and level of use typically achieved by infrastructures' (Plantin and Punathambekar, 2019: 171) or when platforms 'enter more deeply into a variety of infrastructural domains' (Plantin and Punathambekar, 2019) such as urban transport or healthcare (Van Dijck et al, 2018). Importantly, this approach to platforms takes us away from their original definition as open computational systems or programmable architectures. Platforms' scale, indispensability, and level of use are not necessarily functions of their status as programmable architectures but rather pertain to their status as monopolies or very large market actors with sufficient financial power to enter infrastructural domains, sometimes referred to as the 'platformization' of these domains (Poell et al, 2019).

The designed features of the Steam platform can, to some extent, be defined as a 'market infrastructure' in the sense that some of the regulation conventionally maintained by states and regulatory bodies is directly integrated into the platform's material features. One key example is the way Steam defines who can trade what under which circumstances in different parts of the platform. Addressing in this way key platform features as conditions for market interaction allows us to foreground the material aspects of markets as an important area of analysis, which is more or less absent in classic economic and economic-sociological accounts of markets, with a few notable exceptions, such as Garcia-Parpet's famous case study of the Fontaines-en-Sologne strawberry market (Garcia-Parpet, 2007) and Mackenzie's analysis of the material political economy of algorithmic trading (MacKenzie, 2018). However, the current application of the concept of infrastructures in platform studies is so equivocal that the definition of the object of analysis will depend on whether emphasis is put on materiality, scale, or domain of application, and it is not entirely clear if the concept of 'infrastructure' is necessary to conduct this analysis. In Chapter 5, I will demonstrate how the historical development of features on the Steam platform reflects an increased focus on market interactions, and in Chapter 6, I will map how the platform shapes market interactions (Srnicek, 2017) by defining specific rules of transactions (Fligstein 1996, 2001; see also next chapter).

Platform practices

Finally, platforms are approached as a particular domain of practices. This concept has emerged in the field of 'creator cultures' (Burgess, 2021), focusing on the ways platforms shape cultural production. This 'platformisation of cultural content' has been addressed in political-economic analyses (Nieborg and Poell, 2018), while other research has focused on the 'platform practices' shared by creator communities, how these practices shape cultural content, and the platforms themselves (Duffy et al, 2019). Obviously, platforms depend on the participation of content creators and users to transform the platform as an 'environment of expected use' (Light et al, 2018) into actual content and social encounters, and they may take the platform architecture in other directions to what its designers originally aimed for, just as they may inspire platform designers to change the platform architecture in ways that better support its actual use. Though the study I present in the second half of this book does not involve empirical enquiries into the processes of game development and gameplay, it will be an important backdrop to my analysis of the Steam platform economy, not least the development of the Steam platform design as a negotiation between players and publishers as two key groups that sometimes have conflicting interests (see Chapter 5).

In sum, while 'platform' has become a general denominator of the contemporary digital economy, the notion of platforms in practice points towards a wide range of phenomena, from computational systems and multi-sided markets to financial assets and monopolies. Part of the literature dealing with platforms addresses digital games, though the focus of research in this domain has primarily been on standardized computing systems. The large number of approaches and definitions is, of course, a characteristic of most popular terms, and it is perhaps even a necessity in a field traversed by so many different disciplines and methodological approaches. Moreover, it may be due to the fact that the empirical entities we label 'platforms' have also changed over time. To take Facebook as an example, it could probably be meaningfully described as a programmed architecture and an open technology around 2010, yet, in its contemporary form, this is an insufficient description if we are to capture its wider impact on markets and societies. As my colleagues and I argue elsewhere (Thorhauge et al, forthcoming), to fully understand these entities, it is necessary to view them in a broader historical context that allows us to identify the platform in platforms and to assess what should be ascribed to the platform as a standardized computing system and what should be ascribed to wider phenomena or problems such as those monopolies pose to markets across all ages, no matter if the monopolies are held by platform owners or other types of market actors. In the next section, I will try to do this by applying the notion of 'platform configurations' to the way game platforms have developed over time.

Platform configurations in the contemporary game industry

In her comprehensive account of the game industry, Aphra Kerr identifies a number of key trends. These include the diversification of large companies into gaming, the geographical reorganization of the industry with Chinese companies challenging the historical American-Japanese hegemony, and the concentration of ownership in the top five companies in the game industry. Of these, a majority is now from outside the game industry

(Kerr, 2017: 43–4). She observes that 'in 2013 "games only" companies like Activision Blizzard, Take-Two and EA were losing market share while more diversified computer, internet and software companies were gaining' (Kerr, 2017: 52). By 2015, Tencent was the largest public game company and Google and Apple had made their way into the charts (Kerr, 2017: 54). While Sony and Microsoft, key actors in the old console industry, are also diversified companies rather than 'games only' companies, it is fair to say that the old game industry has been disrupted by large platforms referred to as the GAFAM industries (Van Dijck, 2013) and their Chinese counterparts, who now control a majority of the industry. And while both types of industries are dominated by 'platforms', this is in very different ways. The 'platform logics' of proprietary consoles in the 1980s and 1990s involved strategic gatekeeping and close orchestration of software and hardware cycles to increase sales of consoles and game titles in a market dominated by a few platform owners. The 'platform logics' of the GAFAM industries involves the strategic expansion and consolidation of financial control across a wide range of markets. Indeed, as I will return to in the subsequent chapter, this can be described as a movement from 'market power' to 'marketplace power' among these platforms. That is, while console owners would use their control over technologies to maintain a certain hierarchy within the market of digital games, platform companies of the contemporary decade use their financial position to exercise control across a range of markets. Moreover, this development cannot be seen independently of the strategic integration of online distribution and retail on to the business models, another key trend observed by Kerr (2017).

In this way, the 'platform signifier' points to very different types of empirical entities: proprietary technologies for executing video game code or major financial actors owning and controlling large parts of the value chain. If we are to link these highly diverse notions of platforms, it makes more sense to speak of 'platform configurations' including a standardized computing system along with business models, value chains, markets actors, and ownership structures. Kerr's breakdown of the contemporary game industry into five different business segments lends itself well to this approach. As can be seen from Table 2.1, she identifies five business segments in accordance with their business model, software production process, hardware system, and market concentration in terms of business actors. These business segments include proprietary consoles, core computer games, online clients, online applications, and mobile applications, and Kerr primarily addresses these as business clusters with comparable features and approaches. Yet, in the context of the current discussion, they also illustrate well how the platform component serves different roles and involves different kinds of power across the segments interpreted as 'platform configurations'. That is, these segments, with their emphasis on comparable production logics and approaches to business, point towards different ways in which platforms as standardized computing systems are integrated into value chains and market orders across varying types of digital games.

The first segment includes game consoles and the games associated with them. This segment is characterized by proprietary technologies and is dominated by those who own them – Sony, Nintendo, and Microsoft – as well as a few very large publishers like EA and Activision Blizzard (now owned by Microsoft). The consoles are developed as loss leaders (Rochet and Tirole, 2003) and income is generated from game sales. This business segment can be defined as the core of the original game industry market order. Recent decades have primarily brought about a change in retail. While console games can still be purchased in physical retail, they are increasingly downloaded directly from the consoles' digital storefronts, in this way further consolidating the gatekeeping power associated with the console, and somewhat changing the business models towards different sorts of upselling (more about this in the subsequent section). The second segment includes core personal computer games, PC as well as Mac. Apple generally exercises more control over content, yet, as compared to the former segment, this segment is characterized by somewhat more open hardware systems and a larger group of market actors, including Steam. This segment is, similarly, a part of the original game industry market order, representing simultaneously an alternative market for large publishers and a key market for middle-sized and small publishers without access to the core consoles. Like the console games, the business models primarily consist of retail through various sorts of intermediaries.

The two segments of console and core computer games made up the key components of the digital game industry in the 1980s and 1990s. As I will get back to in the subsequent chapter, this can be interpreted as a specific market order, that is, a social field dominated by a few 'incumbents' in the form of console owners and large publishers, and a broad spectrum of middle-sized and small 'challengers', sharing a set of conceptions about expected behaviour and ways of doing business in this field, such as retail as a standard business model (see Chapter 3). Platforms certainly play a key role in this market order, with a strong association between console ownership and market dominance. Yet, there are at least two 'platform configurations' in place already at this point in history. The proprietary consoles represent one such platform configuration represented by a strong concentration of power with the platform owners and a strong linkage between the curation, distribution, and consumption of games. The core computer games represent another type of platform configuration involving more loosely coupled hardware and software systems and, for the same reason, a broader array of market actors specializing in different aspects of the development, distribution, and consumption of digital games. While the platform is easy to define in the case of the game console industry and is truly a key organizing principle in this market segment, it is a much more loosely coupled set of technologies in the case of core computer games and is to a lesser degree the primary organizing principle. Of course, the notion of 'the platform' could be reserved for consoles only, emphasizing, in this way, the ownership structure and the ability to exercise control across the entire value chain. Yet, in this case, it is not the technological principles of the platform itself but rather its position and impact within a wider market context that makes the difference.

While console and core computer games represent the two primary roads into the digital game market throughout the 1980s and 1990s, the popularization of the internet brought about a change in the patterns of game distribution and consumption by enabling the downloading of game titles directly from the publishers' websites and incorporating online gameplay in game design. Obviously, this is not a direct alternative to console and core computer games since games were still being played on computers and, somewhat later, consoles. Online features primarily brought about a change in digital game retail and a new business approach to gaming. As concerns the first, game distribution and game sales moved online and were integrated into the consoles in the form of storefronts. While games in the 1980s and 1990s were purchased in physical retail, they could now be bought and downloaded directly from the publisher or the console. As concerns the second, the initial point of sale characterizing traditional retail was supplemented with a range of additional business strategies including subscription and upselling (more about this in the next section). However, it also gave rise to a third business segment in Kerr's overview based on online clients for game titles, such as the aforementioned MMORPGs and the contemporary multiplayer online battle arenas (MOBAs). These are typically multiplayer game titles with a sufficient following to establish their own 'platform' independently of physical retail and other online storefronts, such as *League of Legends* and *World of Warcraft*. As 'platforms', these clients are not defined by their hardware, which may involve a range of systems; they are applications that enable the execution of the games and handle multiplayer functions, payments, and digital rights management like other platforms do. They are typically made for a specific game title or a number of game titles from the same publisher. Indeed, according to some definitions, such as the literature focusing on 'platform thinking', clients do not really count as platforms since they are not open to third-party developers or publishers but rather feature a one-to-one relationship between game and client. As a platform configuration, they represent a relevant border case, as they integrate a standardized computing system that represents the primary access point to the game; yet, some clients only yield access to game titles from one market actor such as Battle.net, while others offer development and publishing tools for a broad range of actors such as *Roblox*.

Finally, Kerr's fourth and fifth business segments refer to online applications in the form of social networks and browsers and mobile applications on smartphones and tablets. While it makes good sense from Kerr's perspective to distinguish between these, they represent the same sort of platform configuration from the perspective of the current discussion, that is, hardware systems varying with platform and browser and a large number of market actors, with a few becoming dominant. What is also characteristic of these business segments is that they represent a subset in the 'storefronts' of the new tech companies that have entered the digital game industry. The tech companies are in practice 'everything stores' (Stone, 2013) that have integrated digital games in their general strategy of growth and monopolization (Langley and Leyshon, 2017; Srnicek, 2017). This means that these platforms are *primarily* storefronts and secondarily technologies for executing games, typically in the form of additional game services enabling multiplayer gaming. On one hand, this has somewhat opened the market of digital gaming as compared to the console market, allowing a broader array of market actors to publish their games (though Apple upholds comparably higher entry barriers to its storefront). On the other hand, it has concentrated the distribution and sales of game titles, that is, the old retail chain, on the hands of a few gargantuan tech companies.

This story is not very new. Indeed, numerous scholars have addressed the increasing concentration of power on the hands of a few market actors, who have managed to turn themselves into indispensable intermediators across a wide range of market contexts, including digital gaming. Yet, addressing this line of development as an array of varying platform configurations allows us to identify the changing role of platforms as standardized computing systems integrated into market orders, value chains, and ownership structures in a variety of ways. The traditional game console and the large tech company are platforms that in different ways partly concern the platform as a standardized computing system, its position in and integration of the value chain, and the position of the platform owner within the wider market order. While the console game industry, the core of the original market of digital games, used its 'platform power' to maintain high entrance barriers, in this way ensuring a market order dominated by a small number of large market actors and leaving game sales and distribution to physical retail, the large tech companies have lowered these entrance barriers while intensifying their control over distribution and retail, which is now directly integrated into the device and the platform architecture. In the first case, the platform is a technology for executing games; in the second, it is a storefront.

Platform configurations and business models in gaming

The succession of platform configurations discussed previously involves an ongoing development in platform business models from that of publication and retail to that of advertising. At the same time, this development in 'platform logics' shapes the business models of the games published on these platforms. In their work on contingent cultural commodities, Nieborg and Poell address the way processes of platformization shape the production of cultural content (2018). That is, the platform configurations outlined in the previous sections and the different kinds of business logics they entail have profound implications for the way games are produced and circulated. Kerr's overview of business segments indicates as general movement from retail to various sorts of upselling, which is also confirmed by my own data in Chapter 7. Hamari and Järvinen's (2011) description of business models of digital games somewhat mirrors these segments, though they place their attention on the way business models are increasingly embedded into game mechanics. Accordingly, they distinguish between boxed games (the publishing logic of core console and PC games), games as continuous service (the logic of certain client-based games), and free-to-play games (the logics of online and mobile applications and increasingly clients too). Writing in 2011, which is a while ago counted in 'game years', they do not deal with the business models associated with the strategic design of player-driven economies (Lehdonvirta and Castronova, 2014; Thorhauge and Nielsen, 2021; Thorhauge, 2022). However, player-driven economies are, on one hand, an important factor in the strategic design for upselling, and, on the other, a business model in their own right, which will be explored in detail in Chapters 5 to 7. In the following sections, I will firstly describe the movement from classic retail to so-called 'free-to-play' on the basis of Hamari and Järvinen's overview (2011). As an extension of this, I will then address the notion of player-driven economies and how they form the basis for alternative business models.

Boxed content and retail

In the traditional console market, games took the form of boxed content along the same lines as books and films, that is, packaged content sold at a single price at the point of acquisition. Games were produced, packaged, and sold in physical retail to be played on the consoles they were developed for. This market model was, and is to this day, driven forward by interrelated hardware and software cycles, where new consoles boost game sales and key game titles boost the sale of consoles. That is, consoles are released in conjunction with highly profiled game titles to boost sales, while the constant update of consoles, on the other hand, drives the sales of new game titles because games developed for older consoles cannot run on new ones. In this way, tight control over what is published on the platforms to support the interrelated development cycles is key to commercial success, and console owners during the heyday of this market model acted as key gamekeepers limiting access to their platforms (Joseph, 2017: 130; Kerr, 2017). This obviously resulted in high entry barriers and a market dominated by a few console owners and large publishers. The model persists and still makes up an important part of the game business today, with the primary exception that retail has moved online and is to a larger degree controlled by the platforms themselves.

Games as a service and the subscription-based business model

However, as access to the internet became commonplace by the end of the 1990s, new options for distributing and playing games emerged that somewhat disrupted this pattern. On the one hand, players were able to download games rather than buying them in physical retail and, on the other, the internet enabled multiplayer gaming on a large scale, giving online PC gaming a boost. In this way, the turn of the millennium was marked by the advent of massive online multiplayer games, with *Everquest* and *World of Warcraft* as key cases in point. While *Everquest* was published by Sony, one of the key console owners, *World of Warcraft* was published by Blizzard Entertainment, a large game publisher who could in this way distribute its game through its own online client independently of the closed consoles. The MMORPGs by no means replaced the existing market order defined by boxed content and physical retail, but the direct access to audiences and the possibility of cutting physical retail enabled a new type of business model where the game was transformed into a service to which players bought continuous access. That is, instead of paying a single price at the initial point of sale, players would subscribe on a continuous basis to the game world in the same manner as today's streaming services. Hamari and Järvinen (2011) point out that this change affected the way games were designed. While design emphasis in the boxed content model is on initial content, design focus in the subscription model is on long-term engagement. This also means that these types of games have increasingly left the software development cycle that characterized the former market order, and rather exist in a status of 'perpetual beta' (O'reilly, 2007), constantly updating the games in accordance with identified use patterns. While this business model seemed for a while to point towards a whole new direction for the game market, it represents a smaller segment of games today, where social networks and mobile platforms have turned the 'free-to-play' model into 'the most popular prize on the internet' (Hoofnagle and Whittington, 2013).

Mobile gaming and free-to-play

While common access to the internet enabled massive online multiplayer gaming and turned the subscription model into a viable alternative, Facebook's tremendous growth throughout the 2000s as well as the invention and proliferation of smartphones soon turned 'free-to-play' into another widespread business model. In the beginning, these games were titled 'social games' (Hamari and Järvinen, 2011; Lewis et al, 2012) because they were accessed on social media, most notably Facebook. This name is somewhat misleading, since it is not their social features that set them apart from other games but rather that they are 'casual'. That is, they require less time investment and a smaller economic investment at the point of acquisition (though this investment may very well exceed that of traditional games over time). Thus, with the advent of smartphones that made it possible to play in small time intervals at any time and place during the day, these games brought about a 'casual revolution' (Juul, 2010), which radically changed the demographic of gamers. Casual games such as *Angry Birds* and *Candy Crush Saga* broadened the demographic of players with regard to gender and age (Kowert et al, 2017). Facebook is not really a key access point to casual games, as these are primarily accessed via smartphone and tablet storefronts. Yet, the platform still marks a key point in the development of this segment of games, because Facebook's business logics came to define the games published there (Lewis et al, 2012; Nieborg, 2015). In this way, Facebook was important in shaping the development of the free-to-play business model that now dominates casual games across platforms and has increasingly found its way into traditional games. In free-to-play games, the initial point of sale is given up in favour of advertising and upselling. In the first case, players' attention is sold to advertisers; in the second, players are given the option of purchasing additional content. In both cases, Hamari and Järvinen point out, these business logics are integrated into the game mechanics in ways that can maximize time spent on the game (and thus attention sold to advertisers) and incentivize the purchase of additional content.

As concerns ways of making users purchase additional content, business actors within the domain of gaming have developed novel approaches at an astounding pace, and continue to do so (Joseph, 2021; Nieborg, 2021). One of the most debated and indeed infamous ones involves so-called loot boxes, borrowing their mechanics from the domain of gambling. Indeed, the 'formative years' of free-to-play games involved numerous interchanges between actors in gaming and gambling (Cassidy, 2013), meaning that actors in the domain of gambling took inspiration from gaming regarding customer acquisition and actors in the domain of gaming oppositely took inspiration from 'incentivizing' mechanics known from gambling. Thus, loot boxes build on the age-old hope for the 'lucky strike' where you win hundreds, or thousands, of times more than you paid for by pure chance. For instance, you may pay one or two dollars for a key to open a loot box in *Counter-Strike: Global Offensive* and win an item that is valued at more than a thousand dollars in the Steam community market. Of course, this is a very improbable outcome, but urban myth in combination with popular videos on YouTube and Twitch (of which some may be manipulated) add to the impression that this is more probable than it actually is. Depending on the gambling regulation framework and the significance given to the convertibility of stakes and rewards into conventional monetary value (Nielsen and Grabarczyk, 2019), this can be considered direct 'gamblification' of digital games (Johnson and Brock, 2020; Brock and Johnson, 2021; Macey and Hamari, 2022) and has for the same reason spawned a great deal of debate and attempts at regulation (Xiao, 2021).

However, this is not the only way in which the purchase of additional content is incentivized in the domain of gaming. The implementation of 'battle passes' (see Joseph, 2021) across a range of game titles represents an alternative approach which definitely doesn't preclude loot boxes (loot boxes may be part of what you can unlock in a battle pass) but rather builds on the impulse to 'make a deal', that is, to get more virtual goods for your money by purchasing a battle pass than you would have if purchasing the same virtual goods independently of this pass. Thus, once you have purchased a battle pass, you will be rewarded with virtual goods whenever you complete a certain level in the game. Of course, the catch is that you only earn your items if you complete all the levels, and some games offer an option to unlock the rest of your items against an additional payment in case you don't have sufficient time. In this way, the battle pass does not involve any randomization that would classify it as an instance of gambling or gamblified gaming, yet it does represent a relatively manipulative upselling strategy in the domain of free-to-play games, 'a model of commodified play that sits at the intersection of the pay-to-win dynamics of popular mobile games and the gamblification of play' (Joseph, 2021: 69). Indeed, while loot boxes represent a particularly problematic incentivizing game mechanic, they are certainly not the only ones, and in case of the Steam platform and Valve's flagship game title, the integration of loot boxes and random drops into a wider player-driven economy adds another layer to the business model and its wider implications.

Player-driven economies and business models in online gaming

In 2001, Edouard Castronova published a study of the MMORPG *Everquest* as an independent economy (Castronova, 2001). Castronova's reason for publishing this study was his observation that an important part of the attraction of playing *Everquest* was to take part in trading and bargaining with other players, which was a natural result of the specific ways in which resources and dependencies were designed into the game. For instance, Castronova observed that the exchange rate between the in-game currency and dollars was higher than the Japanese yen, the Korean won, and the Italian lira at the time (Castronova, 2008: 19). As I state in the Introduction, the strategic design of game economies is simultaneously an important aspect of the gameplay experience and also, increasingly, part of business models in gaming. Lehdonvirta and Castronova have published a book entirely dedicated to the design and analysis of game economies, from the creation of goods, regulation of markets, and explanations of market power to the design of virtual currencies (Lehdonvirta and Castronova, 2014). To do this, they apply a classic economic perspective focusing on concepts such as supply and demand, exchange mechanisms, and macroeconomic management. At the same time, several of their key concepts are at the core of the free-to-play business models, such as the design of virtual goods and currencies in ways that 'inspire' players to purchase them for conventional money in order to proceed in the game (Hamari and Lehdonvirta, 2010; Hamari and Järvinen, 2011; Lewis et al, 2012; Søraker, 2016).

An important distinction in the design of markets in in-game economies concerns who is able to act as sellers and buyers. While some games only allow players to trade items with non-player characters (instantiations of the game), others allow players to trade items between them and let prices fluctuate accordingly. This creates a much more complex and challenging kind of economy, but it is also more difficult to control and often overlaps with external economies. And while some publishers invest considerable effort into keeping these economies apart, others base their economic rationale on the grey zone between the virtual economy and the conventional economy. This is very likely because player-driven economies, once they gain momentum, can serve as strong dynamos for upselling by increasing demand for items and currencies in the game. While a designer may create a certain demand for items and currencies by designing, for instance, artificial obstacles and intricate dependencies in the game world (Hamari and Järvinen, 2011; Hamari et al, 2017), player-driven economies are a very potent way of sustaining demand for items and currencies and thus drive the upselling part of the business model. Moreover, the overlap between player-driven economies and external economies may lead to alternative business perspectives of interest to the game publisher or platform owner. For instance, the content of loot boxes obtained in certain games on Steam can be resold on the Steam community market, in this way further incentivizing their appeal and integrating them into a more general 'metagame' resting above the level of individual game titles in the tangled markets of the Steam platform.

Platforms, business models, and market orders

In the previous sections, I have addressed the notion of platforms across a range of disciplines and applied it to the way game technologies and platforms have developed in the field of digital games. Moreover, I have described how these changes in platform configurations have affected the business models of digital games. This involves a development from proprietary technological systems in the form of game consoles to large market actors who control large parts of digital game retail by way of their platforms' added storefront features. It also involves a general development from classic retail over various sorts of subscription, advertising, and upselling to the strategic creation of player-driven economies, which will be the focus of this book.

The notion of platforms dominates our conception of contemporary economies. Indeed, it has even been pointed out that platforms are to the digital economy what the factory was to the industrial economy (Kenney and Zysman, 2020). Yet, it covers a wide range of definitions and phenomena, and as this analysis of platform configurations in the domain of digital games indicates, it also changes over time. The concept has somewhat matured with the GAFAM industries (Van Dijck, 2013) from computational architectures to diversified market actors. In this process, focus on the material and programmed characteristics has been replaced with attention on the way these platforms manage to monopolize markets and move into infrastructural domains due to their sheer size. This leads to (at least) two important questions: what difference do the programmed characteristics of the platform make after all, and how should we address those aspects of the platforms that are not functions of their programmed characteristics? As concerns the first question, the programmed characteristics of platforms certainly make a difference. For instance, the coexistence of closed and open platforms in the field of digital games, and the different types and concentration of market actors this involves, indicate that we should definitely pay attention to this component of the platform configuration. However, and this brings us to the second question, this component should be seen as a reflection of wider business models and market orders, which should be taken into consideration as well. While these business models and market orders are not necessarily new to platforms, they are key to understanding the specific ways in which platforms function as market devices. In the subsequent chapter, I will discuss in more detail the relationship between markets and platforms and introduce an economic-sociological perspective on markets as a framework for the ensuing analysis.

Table 2.1: Kerr's overview of key segments in the digital games industry (Kerr, 2017: 39–40)

Segment	Business model	Software production process and development costs	Hardware system	Market concentration
Segment 1 1a Console; 1b Handheld; 1c Console; downloadable (on Xbox Live Aracde (XBLA), PlayStation Network (PSN), WiiWare).	Hardware developed as a loss leader. Game disks sold through retail. DLC sold online/pay per download.	18–48 months to develop – teams of 50–200. Some ongoing support costs. Tens of millions to develop. 1b smaller teams (ten–50) and development costs. 1c cheaper to develop and the smallest teams (5–20).	Closed proprietary technology licensed to developers and content must be approved by platforms.	A few core dominant players with market leader changing during every console lifecycle – currently Sony, Nintendo, Microsoft. A small number of very large publishers like EA and Activision Blizzard. Numerous developers.
Segment 2 2a Core Personal Computer (PC and Mac); 2b PC downloadable.	Retail. Pay per download online distribution through intermediaries and developer websites.	18–24 months – 20–200 teams. Millions to develop. Hundreds of thousands to develop. Small teams of 1–20.	Open. Increasingly using middleware and off-the-shelf engines and tools.	Numerous players, for example, Firaxis, CD Projekt, id Software, Bethesda Game Studios. Thousands of small companies like Mojang and intermediaries like Steam.
Segment 3 Online clients (especially MMO and MOBA).	Monthly subscription, pay-to-play. Freemium/ free-to-play.	48 months – 100–200 teams. Tens of millions to develop and ongoing servicing costs.	Open.	A small number of large players, for example, Activision Blizzard, NetEase, Riot, Wargaming, and CCP.
Segment 4 Online applications (social networks and browsers).	Freemium, advertising, and data-supported microtransactions.	12 months – 12–20 people. Service costs more than one million.	Varies by platform and browser.	Numerous, but a small number becoming dominant: Tencent, Webzen, Facebook, EA, Amazon, Zynga.
Segment 5 Mobile applications (smartphones, tablets).	Freemium, pay-per-download, advertising, and data-supported microtransactions.	Three months but increasing. Small teams, less than one million, but growing.	Varies by platform – closed with App Store, more open with Google Play and others.	Numerous – Tencent, Apple, Google, Rovio, King, Zynga, GungHo, Disney, Apple, EA, NetEase, Supercell.

3

Economic Sociology and the Analysis of Platforms as Markets

In the previous chapter, I observed how the notion of platforms has changed throughout recent decades from signifying a computational system (Bogost and Montfort, 2009) or a programmable architecture (Van Dijck et al, 2018) to a more general principle of organization (Kenney and Zysman, 2020; Stark and Pais, 2020) and a business model aimed at cornering markets and reaching monopoly status (Langley and Leyshon, 2017; Srnicek, 2017; Peck and Phillips, 2020). This can be related somewhat to the general transformation of platform companies and market orders during this time span, such as the change in the game industry from a market order dominated by a few console owners to one dominated by large tech companies from outside the gaming industry. While the platform as a computational system or programmable architecture is easily identified as the key principle of power in a market order controlled by console owners, the large tech companies control the market through their storefronts or extended market places (Doyle, 2013) and through their financial power to dominate the entire market field. One significant theme that runs through this course of development is the integration of retail into platform architectures, and the increasing focus on platforms as markets. Thus, another aspect of platforms which is often foregrounded is that they constitute multi-sided markets (Rochet and Tirole, 2003; Evans and Schmalensee, 2016; Van Dijck et al, 2018) that let different groups of customers meet on attractive terms. The aim of this chapter is to interrogate more systematically what this aspect of platforms involves. Are platforms primarily to be understood as multi-sided markets or do they integrate market components to various extents? Are all interactions taking place on platforms to be considered market interactions or is this classification reserved for specific types of interaction on platforms? And does the notion of multi-sided markets sufficiently address complex market constructions of platforms such as Steam?

In the subsequent sections, I will firstly take a closer look at the notion of multi-sided markets in platform studies. As an extension of this, I will describe and discuss how markets should be defined, as this concept is taken more or less for granted across disciplines. I will introduce an economic-sociological perspective on markets to address what characterizes them in comparison with other types of economic organization, and to define markets as fields populated by 'incumbents' and 'challengers' who act strategically to maintain or challenge a certain market order. I then return to the notion of platforms as multi-sided markets on the basis of this framework to clarify some of the ambiguities with regard to the relationship between markets and platforms. To do this, I introduce the concept of 'tangled markets', that is, a set of interconnected and mutually dependent market contexts. This concept does not replace or oppose that of multi-sided markets but rather addresses the 'entanglement' of market contexts on the Steam platform and the way this can be considered a core principle in the value extraction mechanism of Steam.

The market in platform studies

The notion of the platform as a market returns in several definitions of platforms in critical platform studies. Srnicek points out that one key feature of the platform is its ability to set the rules for production and service development as well as market interactions: 'Uber, despite presenting itself as an empty vessel for market forces, shapes the appearance of a market' (2017: 47). Van Dijck et al state that 'Connective platforms are dependent on "complementors" – organisations or individuals that provide products or service to end users through platforms, interlinking different "sides" and hence constituting multi-sided markets' (2018: 17), referencing Evans and Schmalensee's work on multi-sided markets (2016). Evans and Schmalensee contrast multi-sided platforms with ordinary businesses that merely aim to attract customers to sell them goods on profitable terms: 'Multi-sided platforms, in contrast, need to attract two or more types of customers by enabling them to interact with each other on attractive terms. Their most important inputs are generally their customers" (2016: 15). While they state that the business model was discovered in 2000 with Rochet and Tirole's work on platform competition in multi-sided markets (2003), many of their illustrations predate this year. Indeed, reading their and Rochet and Tirole's work, it is not entirely clear what exactly should be put into their notion of platforms. While software and internet-based services certainly make up a large share of their examples, they also include credit card companies, social gatherings, shopping malls, and real estate (2003: 992). Indeed, their focus is primarily on the *business model*, while the platform can take a range of shapes, which are increasingly digital. In his book on platform economies, Marc Steinberg similarly address how 'transactional platforms' are in fact 'a-technological' though historically coinciding with a range of digital technologies (2019). He foregrounds several Japanese scholars, Kokuryoo Jiroo, Kimura Makoto, and Negoro Tatsuyuki (2019: 109), who come to similar conclusions as Evans and Schmalensee and Rochet and Tirole ten years ahead of them, although from a slightly different perspective. While their western counterparts place their emphasis on microeconomics, industrial economics, and price formation in multi-sided markets, these scholars, writing in the tradition of business management, take more interest in platforms as intermediaries and enablers of trust across a range of contexts, including digital ones.[1] From this perspective, the notion of the platform rather replaces the notion of the 'firm' as an organizing principle, further emphasizing how this is to a lesser degree a question of the specific programmable architecture on which this market is based and more a question of organizing market interactions in new ways.

Thus, platforms as multi-sided markets are not necessarily defined by their technology but rather by the way in which they organize market interactions. The other way around, it is not entirely clear if digital platforms are always to be considered multi-sided markets and whether all interaction taking place on digital platforms should be considered market interactions. While platforms like Amazon Marketplace, Uber, and Airbnb can certainly be defined as markets where products and services are exchanged by way of economic transactions, the 'market' of platforms like Facebook, YouTube, and Google, that is, their associated advertising markets, lingers in the background of the primary activities these platforms offer their users: social networking, streaming, and internet search. Are these activities, then, also market interactions or are they non-market interactions that are subsequently monetized in auxiliary markets? In their early work on two-sided markets, Eisenmann et al do seem to include consumers and searchers as 'market sides' on advertisement-driven platforms such as Miami Yellow Pages and web search (2006: 4). However, a more precise designation of users in these contexts would be 'audience commodities' (Smythe, 1981; Manzerolle, 2010; Fuchs, 2014; see also Chapter 9), that is, they are not market actors, they are the good that is being exchanged.

The notion of platforms as multi-sided markets certainly makes sense in the case of the game market, where digital platforms have integrated retail and, in this way, effectively function as 'matchmakers' (Evans and Schmalensee, 2016) between game publishers and game players. However, other scholars are opposed to the notion of platforms as multi-sided markets. Stark and Pais (2020) define a platform as a distinct organizational form that differs from that of markets, hierarchies, and networks: 'whereas for markets the verb is "contract", the verb for hierarchies is "command" and for networks is "collaborate" … platforms "co-ops" assets that are not part of the firm and create value in a social and economic space that is neither inside nor outside the platform' (2020: 48). As Ørmen and Gregersen (forthcoming) point out, this description recalls some of the key points of resource dependence theory (Pfeffer and Salancik, 2003), that is, firms' strategic attempts to control key resources in their environments. Platforms acquire resources that they do not own and manage users that are not their employees by way of algorithmic management in the form of ratings, rankings, and visibility. For instance, Airbnb does not own the accommodation facilities offered on the platform, and the lessors are not their employees. Still, they manage these resources by way of algorithmic management.

Other scholars emphasize that platforms are not just markets in their own right but folded 'markets' (Vonderau, 2019), and they are assets and actors in wider financial markets (Langley and Leyshon, 2017; Srnicek, 2017). While they may represent markets in a direct and indirect sense, they simultaneously play into the logics of financial capitalism. Vonderau (2019) defines Spotify as a folded market as an extension of this train of thought. While Spotify may present itself to its users as a music service, a market of music publishers and music listeners, the company is registered in public markets of interest as a 'tech company' to advance its financial value, and its 'metrics' serve to boost its value as a financial asset as much as they truly represents its value as a market and a service. Thus, it makes little sense to analyse Spotify and its public reporting without considering its double role as a music service and a financial asset in the stock market. Relatedly, Langley and Leyshon point out that platforms' specific business arrangements are incorporated into wider processes of capitalization, that is, 'they perform the structure of the venture capital funds that are the major source of investment in platforms' (2017). Indeed, Srnicek points out that one key to understanding the current power of platforms resides in the concentration of private money after the financial crisis in 2008 and loose financial politics that enabled the astronomic growth of certain financial actors (2017). From this perspective, platforms are not influential due to their 'platform thinking' or because they have found a better way for implementing multi-sided markets but due to their financial power. This has led Peck and Phillips to define platforms, basically, as 'antimarket' (2020). Applying Fernand Braudel's notion of the 'antimarket' to their analysis of contemporary platforms, they find them to be 'new machines for the concentration of power and the monopolization of markets', that is, the opposite of the ideal of competitive markets and perhaps the true nature of capitalism.

Part of this disagreement over platforms' status as markets can, of course, be explained with the level of analysis. Platforms can be programmed architectures that enable market interactions at the same time as their owners are market actors with potentially monopolistic and anti-competitive strategies. However, this also pertains to a lack of explanation of the relationship between platforms and markets; *are* platforms markets or do they display market features? Are platforms markets to varying degrees? And what do we even mean when we talk about markets? The latter question must be addressed before the first two can be answered. In the following sections, I will firstly identify theoretical traditions that have dealt with markets and their key features. Next, I will address Karl Polanyi's monumental work on the market society, and his notions of economic organization, fictitious commodities, embeddedness, and the role of the state. After this, I will address in more detail how more recent work in market sociology has approached markets as institutions and social orders. Finally, I will return to the notion of platforms as markets and argue that digital platforms can certainly be defined as markets, though they may display different degrees of 'marketness'. Furthermore, several major platforms addressed in the field of critical platform studies, including the Steam platform, should rather be addressed as 'tangled markets' that find their business logic at the intersection between markets they control by way of their platforms.

Approaches to markets within classic economics and economic sociology

In the introduction to his book *Marketcraft* subtitled *How Governments Make Markets Work* (2018), Steven Vogel states that:

> a perfect market would have many buyers and sellers, comparable products, complete information, no enforcement costs, and supply and demand would determine prices. This volume focuses on real world markets, not perfect markets, so it defines 'markets' simply as arenas where buyers and sellers come together to exchange goods and/or services. (2018: 11)

In this way, Vogel distinguishes between 'the market' as an abstract idea and 'markets' as real-world contexts where real-world exchanges are made in ways that do not necessarily align with the ideals of the perfect market. Patrick Aspers defines a market as:

> a social structure for the exchange of rights in which offers are evaluated and priced, and compete with one another, which is shorthand for the fact that actors – individuals and firms – compete with one another via offers. This definition covers the market as a place, as well as markets as institutions. (2011: 4)

Aspers includes the notion of competition, a key aspect of the classic market ideal, and also makes a slightly different distinction, that is, between markets as places and markets as institutions, indicating that both specific marketplaces, such as Airbnb, and the more general market of temporary accommodation are included in the definition. Both authors write within traditions of economic sociology and political science that challenge the classic economic ideal of perfect markets, hence Vogel's emphasis on real-world markets and Aspers' focus on social structures. In this way, most of the literature I will deal with in this chapter challenges the classic economic notion of the market and suggests alternative, empirically grounded explanations of markets and how they work. As the subtitle of Vogel's volume indicates, much of this literature also challenges the idea that markets and states are opposites and generally emphasizes the amount of political and social regulation that goes into creating and maintaining markets in opposition to the classic economic ideal. Given the wide use of this ideal, it has been surprisingly difficult to find that one authoritative source that defines it, and most popularized approaches are occupied with its features: it should be free, non-regulated, offer perfect information and competition, and so on, but how the classic market is *defined* except for, most basically, a context of economic exchange is difficult to ascertain. I will base my analysis on theories that define markets as political fields and institutions (Fligstein, 1996, 2001) and social orders (Beckert, 2009) where a range of actors create alliances and continuously negotiate their positions in an ongoing process of 'dynamic disequilibrium' (Beckert, 2009). An important forerunner to this line of thought is Karl Polanyi, who published his analysis of the rise of the market society in 1944.

The rise of the market society and the notion of embeddedness

Polanyi's *The Great Transformation* (1944) is a key reference in economic sociology. In this monumental work, he maps the rise of the market society, beginning with mercantilism and the formation of the nation state, and discusses the institutional characteristics and societal consequences of the emerging market. His work, according to Krippner, 'aims to counter the tendency of economists to project categories and concepts developed to explain specific features of modern Western societies across history and across cultures' (2001: 781). Thus, Polanyi put great effort into demonstrating how trade and economic action in earlier times differed fundamentally from those of the contemporary market. He rejects the Smithsonian idea that the market can be traced back to man's 'propensity to barter, truck and exchange one thing for another' (1944: 45)[2] and challenges the notion of an evolutionary line going from local barter over regional and national trade to today's global markets. He argues that local as well as global trade existed centuries ahead of modern markets as extensions of local communities and global politics, but these economic activities did not constitute markets in the classic economic sense of the word; they were 'embedded' into the social and political relationships of the involved actors and served to confirm and reproduce the relationships of these actors rather than constituting an independent realm of economic interaction. Market society rather came into being with the rise of the nation state in the 18th century. Polanyi emphasizes the key role of the nation state in the construction of the free market, which was nothing less than 'an institutional separation of society into an economic and a political sphere' (1944: 74). In the following, I will limit myself to three concepts that play a key role in my analysis in this as well as the coming chapters: the organization of economic action, the embeddedness of economic action, and the concept of fictitious commodities.

As concerns the organization of economic action, Polanyi compares the market as a specific way of organizing economic action with its alternatives. This is sometimes referred to as a three-tier categorization into reciprocity, redistribution, and markets (Krippner, 2001: 779; Stark and Pais, 2020: 49). However, Polanyi in fact includes a fourth alternative, that of householding (1944: 57). While reciprocity is primarily related to family and kinship, 'redistribution is mainly effective in relation to all those who are under a common chief and is, therefore, of a territorial character' (1944: 50). Thus, a reciprocal organization of economic action involves that people exchange goods with their peers with the expectation that they will be compensated with the reciprocal exchange of other goods, and redistribution involves that all goods are shared in a common storage from where they are redistributed. This redistribution is not necessarily even, as feudal societies illustrate. As concerns householding, 'the forgotten principle', this concerns the production of goods for the self-sufficient household (1944: 56). What these principles have in common is that they 'are a mere function of social organization' (1944: 52) of kinship, tribe, and household. In the market, however, economic action has been 'disembedded' from these social structures to constitute its own sphere of action.

Thus, Polanyi's account of market society and his concept of embeddedness concerns the historical process in which economic action is institutionally separated into its own sphere that exists independently of the social structures of which it used to be part. Moreover, this new sphere of economic interaction grew in importance and exerted increased power over other aspects of society, that is, 'instead of the economy being embedded in social relations, social relations are embedded in the economy' (1944: 60). While feudal power set the rules for economic exchange in medieval societies, economic exchange set the rules for the rest of market society. Of course, this state of affairs is never absolute, and Polanyi describes social history in the 19th century as a double movement:

While on the one hand markets spread all over the globe and the amount of goods involved grew to unbelievable dimensions, on the other hand a network of measures and policies was integrated into powerful institutions designed to check the action of the market relative to labour, land and money. (1944: 79)

The market makes inroads into society and society responds with various measures to mitigate the detrimental consequences.

The notion of embeddedness has played a key role in the formation of new economic sociology as a field. In his seminal work on 'the problem of embeddedness' (1985), Granovetter reactivates the notion of embeddedness in his attempt to create a middle ground between what he defines as sociology's over-socialization and economy's under-socialization of the individual. He refers to Dennis Wrong's (1961) critique of modern sociology's tendency to over-socialize individuals, that is, to reduce their action to a function of the social structures of which they are part, while in contrast, Granovetter argues, classical and neoclassical economics operate with an atomized and under-socialized notion of human action. However, Granovetter points out:

Actors do not behave or decide as atoms outside a social context, nor do they adhere slavishly to a script written for them by the particular intersection of social categories that they happen to occupy. Their attempts at purposive action are instead embedded in concrete, ongoing systems of social relations. (1985: 487)

In this way, Granovetter uses 'the embeddedness argument', the observation that economic actors are always 'embedded' into social networks and their economic actions are therefore conditioned by these, to make a case for the analysis of economic actors' social networks instead. Later works, most notably Krippner (2001), Beckert (2007), and Krippner and Alvarez (2007), have questioned Granovetter's use of 'embeddedness', pointing out that it 'represents an inversion of the original concept' (Krippner, 2001: 777). While Polanyi uses the concept to examine institutions that structure empirical economies, Granovetter uses it to abstract away from the complexities this implies and focuses on a single aspect: the configuration of network ties. As Krippner and Alvarez point out in a later publication, the two approaches represent 'fundamentally different conceptions of the relationship between the economic and the social' (2007: 431), which I interpret to concern the separation of social and economic action at an institutional level (Polanyi) and the intersection between economic and social action at the level of social networks (Granovetter). My analysis of Steam's value extraction mechanism in Chapter 4 makes a case for the combination of the two approaches, where the 'Polanyian' notion of embeddedness can be used to explain the disembedding of the economic relations of player communities into market relations as a way of converting affective value into market value, while the 'Grannovetterian' emphasis on the network ties of economic actors can explain how the ongoing economic action on Steam remains 'embedded' into those gaming communities that create the value in the first place. Before I pass on to this part of the analysis, I will explain one final concept in Polanyi's original framework, that of the 'fictitious commodity'.

Fictitious commodities,[3] in Polanyi's term, are resources that are not created as goods but are transformed into goods by way of the market. Polanyi ties this concept to the characteristics of industrial production and the factory system, which involve long-term investment and corresponding risk, and hence demand stable access to necessary resources to ensure continued production. The most important ones are land, labour, and money, and according to Polanyi, 'their supply could be organised in one way only, by being made available for purchase … as commodities' (1944: 78). What renders these goods fictitious is that they are created for different purposes. For instance, people don't have children with the primary purpose of supplying the industrial production chain. Yet, 'the fiction of [land, labour, and money] being so produced became the organising principle of society' (Polanyi, 1944: 79). Of the three types of fictitious commodities Polanyi lists, money is the most challenging. It seems rather straightforward that land and labour exist before and independently of the market and must be adapted to it, but it seems less straightforward that money has its own existence in the same way. Indeed, one could argue that money is, more than anything, a 'creature of the market'. When Polanyi includes money as a fictitious commodity, it may be due to the transformation of money itself from a unit of exchange to an investment asset (see Chapter 8). Nevertheless, the notion of fictitious commodities is very useful for understanding how our lifeworld in the age of digital connectivity is turned into a fictitious commodity.

Markets as institutions: stability and change

As mentioned in the previous section, Polanyi is concerned with 'the economy as an instituted process' (2001: 779), that is, how the economy is organized in society by way of an ongoing process of institutionalization. Later work in the sociology of markets has taken up this challenge, identifying markets as fields (Fligstein, 2001) where actors handle coordination problems through strategic interaction (Beckert, 2009). In the following, I will focus on Fligstein's (Fligstein, 1996, 2001) notion of markets as fields where incumbent firms act strategically to stabilize their position vis-à-vis challenger firms. While Fligstein puts his primary emphasis on the strive for social stability, Beckert's (2009) notion of coordination problems in markets accounts for the opposite, that is, dynamic processes of market change.

The core materials for Fligstein's theory about markets was published in his article on markets as politics (1996). The notion of politics in this context points to both the 'formation of markets as modern state building' (1996: 657) and power struggles in the market, including those that go on inside and across firms. In the article, he lists the key features of his theory, including the components of 'market institutions', the role of the 'state' in market building, the distinction between 'incumbents' and 'challengers', and, last but not least, the assertion that strategic action should be seen as attempts to 'mitigate the effects of competition' with other firms (Fligstein, 1996). Indeed, while most of the market definitions I have addressed until now have defined themselves in opposition to the classic economic ideal, while at the same time somewhat repeating it (Krippner, 2001), Fligstein questions the most basic assumption in the classic economic notion of markets: that markets are competitive. In his book on the architecture of markets from 2001 (republished in 2018), he primarily fleshes out the key proposition of his 1996 article and adds his frameworks of field theory. Thus, while his 1996 article built on Harrison White's work on production markets (1981) and DiMaggio and Powell's study on organizational fields (1983), his book addresses markets on the basis of this somewhat more general theory of social fields.

Fligstein generally envisions markets as social fields inhabited by 'incumbents and challengers' (2001: 76) who compete and cooperate in accordance with certain 'conceptions of control', which I will get back to in a moment. Markets can be in states of emergence, stability, or crisis (Fligstein, 2001: 75), which greatly affect the relationship between incumbents and challengers. While a stable market is typically dominated by a few incumbents who orient themselves towards each other and act strategically to maintain the given order, markets in emergence are more fluid and the roles of incumbents and challengers are yet to be defined. Similarly, markets in crisis are more susceptible to transformation. Due to incumbents' investment in the given order, changes and crises will typically be induced from outside the market and typically from 'nearby' markets (Fligstein, 2001: 84). Applied to the historic development of platforms and market orders addressed in the previous chapter, this involves the development from a relatively stable market in which game console owners are the primary incumbents to a new market field where Big Tech companies have taken the role as incumbents. This transformation has clearly come from the 'nearby market' of technology companies, though it is not clear-cut. Microsoft takes a key position in both market orders and the incumbents of the previous market order remain important, now as key players in a specific segment of console games and core PC games (Kerr, 2017).

Fligstein defines the basic components of this market institution as property rights, governance structures, conceptions of control, and rules of exchange

(Fligstein, 1996: 658; 2001: 32–3). Of these, conceptions of control are the most complex. They are closely tied to the two 'control' projects of firms to handle the power struggles inside the firm and recognize 'the social stabilizing effects of the current relations between firms' (2001: 69). In this way, the conception of control can be summarized as 'market-specific agreements between actors in firms on principles of internal organization … tactics for competition or cooperation … and the hierarchy or status ordering of firms in a given market' (2001: 35). Or, more plainly: 'a story about what the organization is and its location vis-à-vis its principal competitors' (2001: 69). As an example, Fligstein mentions that:

> one common conception of control in high-technology markets is the attempt to make one's product an industry standard. This is a tricky thing to do. If one tries to be too proprietary about creating a particular standard, other firms will resist. In order to produce a standard, one must make the standard open to all potential users. A firm that is fortunate enough to have its technology be adopted as the industry standard can be characterized as having a kind of monopoly. (2001: 72)

In this way, firms may use their control over certain technologies to promote a certain 'conception of control' across the market, for instance, by making it open enough to ensure broad adoption. In this way, the notion of platform and platform power, as addressed in the field of platform studies, finds its corresponding concept in the notion of 'industry standards'. Addressing in this way platforms as industry standards allows us to interpret platform power as a specific conception of control that persists through the dominance of a given technology as well as other market actors' willingness to accept this as an industry standard. It cannot be reduced to any of these. In the market order dominated by owners of game consoles, consoles and PCs represented the industry standard; in the market order dominated by the GAFAM industries, these platforms represent the industry standard. As concerns the other components of the market institutions, Fligstein emphasizes the key role of the state in the constitution of property rights, governance structures, and rules of exchange (2001: 41). Governance structure in this framework covers law as well as informal institutional practices, while rules of exchange 'define who can transact with whom and the conditions under which transactions are carried out' (Fligstein, 1996: 658). In my analysis of the Steam platform features in Chapter 6, I will demonstrate how these rules of transactions are designed into different aspects of the system.

As mentioned previously, Fligstein counters most common sense definitions of markets by stating that the primary purpose of social organization in markets is to mitigate the consequences of competition (1996: 657). That is, 'entrepreneurs and managers construct their actions so as to avoid price competition and stabilize their position vis-à-vis other competitors' (Fligstein, 2001: 71). This is because the goal of strategic economic action is ultimately not competition but the survival of the firm. Internally, firms control competition by way of integration, such as strategic acquisition, and diversification. They may also form alliances with other firms so that 'a few firms can control the market by tacitly agreeing not to threaten one another's position through a price war' (2001: 73). For instance, the old market order of console and PC games can to some degree be interpreted as an alliance or 'coopetition' between game console owners and large publishers, while the diversification strategies of contemporary Big Tech can be interpreted as an alternative approach to handle the threat of competition. As I will get back to in my analyses of market actors operating on the Steam platform in Chapter 7, the presence and absence of specific market actors indicate the current market order, including companies' current attempts to capture the industry standard of PC games.

In my introduction to Fligstein, I put a certain emphasis on exactly when the different parts of his theory were published. I do this because of his emphasis on stability and his claim that:

> since the worldwide economic depression of the 1930s and the devastation of World War II, the world's capitalist economies have grown incredibly as governments learned how to stabilize markets by regulation, controlling the money supply, fiscal policy, and mediating in interfirm relations and worker-firm relations ... since the 1930s, there have been no large-scale worldwide depressions. (2001: 90)

This citation reflects that his framework is developed well before the financial crisis of 2007 and the global recession that followed it. In this way, the notion of 'safeguarding man' (Sparsam, 2016), which pervades his approach to markets as fields, may just be another 'perception of control' reflected in his particular interpretation of market actors. Indeed, the inclination to 'move fast and break things', as reflected in Taplin's portait of Silicon Valley companies (2017), may represent an alternative and somewhat conflicting 'conception of control' in Fligstein's framework. Thus, even though Fligstein does account for different market phases, his notion that change is primarily initiated from outside markets is insufficient. Beckert (2009), on the other hand, addresses the notion of competition and change inside markets as a 'dynamic disequilibrium' (2009: 262). He states that markets as social systems face three coordination problems: the value problem, the problem of competition, and the cooperation problem, 'which can only be resolved if market actors are able to form stable expectations with regard to the actions of other market actors' (2009: 247), in line with Fligstein's train of thought. However, he points out, 'the co-existence of stable worlds and uncertainty is an unavoidable state of affairs in capitalist economies and an indispensable precondition for their dynamics' (2009: 261). He bases this claim on the empirical observation that capitalist economies expand, innovate, and constantly create uncertainty, as well as the theoretical observation that in markets where risk was totally calculable, profit would not be possible. Thus, he describes the balance between reduced uncertainty through embeddedness and the simultaneous preservation of uncertainty as a 'dynamic disequilibrium' (2009: 262) and traces the sources of uncertainty to continuous innovation, competition, institutional contradictions, and human creativity: 'in capitalist economies, the complex embeddedness of markets comes up against actors' motivations to find new ways to secure profits or utility, and contradictory institutional configurations that lead to a continual challenging of existing institutions, networks, products and technologies by innovation' (2009: 263).

In sum, while classic economy's notion of perfect markets is what typically comes to mind when the idea of markets is invoked, Polanyi's account of the rise of market society as well as later work in market sociology draw a more complex picture of what markets are. Markets are not the only way of organizing economic action, but they are a defining feature of the way economic action is organized in market societies. Market societies have emerged by way of a process in which economic action and the social structures into which they used to be embedded have been institutionally separated. The process is not absolute, however, and a double movement persists where markets make inroads into society and society responds with countermeasures. Thus, markets as contexts of economic exchange are socially embedded. Moreover, they are institutionally separated fields defined by a number of actors that coordinate their actions in order to retain a stable world, while the 'dynamic disequilibrium' of capitalism means that uncertainty persists. In the next section, I will apply these insights to the question I asked in the beginning, that is, the ways platforms can be considered markets.

Tangled markets

In the introductory sections of this chapter, I asked what markets were, in what ways platforms could be considered markets, and if they could be considered markets in different ways. While the former sections hopefully answer the first question to some extent, that is, markets are institutionally separate fields of economic exchange in which market actors coordinate their actions, I will now turn to the second and third questions. To set the frame for this discussion, a few simple distinctions should firstly be made. One is the distinction between the platform and the platform owner, that is, the service and the company that owns it. This distinction is so straightforward that it may be considered directly banal. Nevertheless, the two are very often confused, leading to a range of misunderstandings. For instance, does Facebook as a platform constitute a monopoly and, if so, in which market? Or does Meta, through its ownership of the Facebook and Instagram platforms, control an unreasonably large part of the market of advertising in certain contexts of the world? I would say the latter. Another distinction is the one between the market as a specific context of economic exchange and the market as a general institution, as suggested by Aspers (2011). For instance, the Steam game store represents a specific marketplace for PC games which is part of the wider market for these games, encompassing game stores on competing platforms as well as online and physical retail (or, what is left of it). Again, while this distinction may seem banal, it is important because it defines the ways in which we talk about platforms and markets.

Multi-sided markets and tangled markets

Platforms like Uber and Airbnb certainly constitute markets as institutionally separate fields in which market actors coordinate their actions. Moreover, they map neatly on to the concept of multi-sided markets 'that attract two or more types of customers by enabling them to interact with each other on attractive terms' (Evans and Schmalensee, 2016: 15). Uber and Airbnb enable the interaction between buyers and sellers of car rides and temporary accommodation respectively. However, the *primary* services of Facebook and YouTube, social networking and streaming platforms, do not fit the notion of multi-sided markets very well. While these platforms do display certain characteristics of multi-sided markets, they cannot be reduced to these markets as the majority of their users do not access the platforms as market actors but as users of these services. I deliberately put *primary* in italics here because Facebook and YouTube do display transactional affordances (Manzerolle and Daubs, 2016; Manzerolle and Daubs, 2021) that enable direct market interactions between users, for instance, Facebook's marketplace. Moreover, a range of market actors or complementors (Van Dijck et al, 2018) use these platforms to extend their businesses in a number of ways, such as restaurants and shops staying in touch with their customers, introducing a range of additional market contexts to the platforms. However, from the perspective of advertising, the main business model of both platforms, it is less clear if audiences and advertisers represent customers in the same sense as the buyers and sellers on Uber and Airbnb, or, at least, whether it is analytically beneficial to put it this way. While Eisenmann et al (2006) seem to think along these lines, from the perspective of the platform owner, they are the commodity which is being exchanged. To use a very old-fashioned terminology, Facebook and YouTube are 'attention factories' that produce audience commodities (Smythe, 1981; see also Chapter 9), which are then sold in the associated market of advertising.

The concept of multi-sided markets only partly explains this aspect of advertisement-based platforms, with its emphasis on market actors and how their interactions are organized by way of the platform design. For the purpose of the forthcoming analysis, I will suggest the concept of 'tangled markets' to address the entanglement of different markets and domains of interaction on digital platforms. Tangled markets can be defined as complex market contexts containing several interconnected and mutually dependent markets and domains of interaction. The concept is not in opposition to multi-sided markets and does not replace it. It speaks to an aspect of digital platforms that is not sufficiently addressed in the framework of multi-sided markets. For instance, the market for Facebook advertising constitutes its own context where economic transactions take place between the platform owner and advertisers, and interaction on the platform is deeply intertwined with this advertising logic. Indeed, the way the platform shapes cultural production on these platforms turns the business strategies of individual entrepreneurs into vehicles of this logic (Nieborg, 2015; Nieborg and Poell, 2018; Duffy et al, 2019). That is to say, the market interactions between users and between users and complementors are *embedded* into the advertising market of Facebook. They appear at the same time as market contexts in their own right and as components in Facebook's tangled market. In this way, to analyse Facebook as a market context it is not sufficient to identify the different 'market sides' (Eisenmann et al, 2006) and their terms of interaction; it is also necessary to address the *entanglement* of these market contexts and how they condition each other.

The analysis of the Steam platform as a tangled market

Games can serve as 'attention factories' in the same manner as other advertisement-driven entertainment. This is the case in terms of advertisement-based games, typically within platform configurations of online and mobile games (Kerr, 2017), as has been addressed in detail by Nieborg (2015, 2016). However, on the Steam platform, advertising is directly rejected as a revenue model and the microtransaction system is promoted as the preferred alternative. Its business model is based on the interplay between various contexts of economic exchange, from the classic multi-sided market of the games store over the integration of microtransactions into different aspects of the platform to the third-party websites that offer trading and gambling with items from Steam-based games. For this reason, the Steam platform represents a very distinctive type of tangled market. Games are exchanged as commodities in the context of the game store but simultaneously function as additional market contexts where virtual economies blend with real market interactions, and items obtained in these games are traded in 'secondary markets' (Lehdonvirta and Castronova, 2014) on and beyond the platform. Users on the steam platform are simultaneously addressed as consumers, traders, and, indeed, labourers. As compared to the 'attention factories' of Facebook and YouTube, games on the Steam platform can be analysed as 'affection factories' eagerly run by dedicated gamer communities. The affection generated in gaming contexts, often expressed as affectional value attached to items, characters, and players, is monetized through the conversion of affectional value into market value by way of microtransactions across a range of contexts.

In the analytical chapters, I will substantiate and elaborate this claim through a systematic analysis of the way Steam's business model has developed over time and is currently reflected in the platform design. Moreover, I will map and discuss how market actors on and beyond the platform transform these features into business strategies in ways that serve the economic interests of the platform owner. The theorical concepts presented in the current chapter will frame this analysis in a range of ways. In Chapter 5, I will demonstrate how the historical development of the Steam platform's business model can be interpreted as a gradual change of business emphasis from the classic multi-sided market of the game store to the monetization of player-driven economies in alternative contexts of economic exchange. I will define this value extraction mechanism as a case of 'dispossession by disembedment', with reference to Polanyi's distinction between different types of economic organization and his notion of embeddedness as the way in which economic exchange is embedded into social structures in non-market contexts. I will argue that the integration of the microtransactions system into alternative contexts of the platform implies a reorganization of player communities as defined by tribe and kinship into market interaction, and thus a conversion of the affective value residing in player communities into market value that can be exchanged and leveraged for other purposes. In Chapter 6, I will map how this value extraction mechanism is effectuated by the platform design and the different contexts of economic exchange enabled by the platform, and describe how they effectively demarcate the 'rules of transaction', as defined by Fligstein (Fligstein, 1996, 2001). In Chapter 7, I will address the way in which different types of market actors operating on the platform transform these affordances (Hutchby, 2001) into actual business emphases. I will apply Fligstein's notion of market fields populated by incumbents and challengers to demonstrate how the market order on Steam reflects the wider market order of which Steam is part, and how 'incumbents' and 'challengers' position themselves on the platform. Finally, in Chapter 8, I will demonstrate how this tangled market cannot be limited to the platform itself but intersects with a range of economic practices beyond it that serve to consolidate and propagate the overall platform economy.

4

Valve Corporation and the Steam Platform

In the next four chapters, I will provide an empirically grounded analysis of the Steam platform as a particular type of game platform. I will do this because the Steam platform exhibits a distinct platform business model rooted in the economic features of games. Steam is, on one hand, comparable to other market platforms, with its focus on attracting game publishers and gamer communities into a multi-sided market controlled by the platform owner. On the other hand, it differs from other platforms in its active integration of player-driven economies at different levels of its platform design. This turns Steam into a direct illustration of the way platforms can be defined and analysed as 'tangled markets', extracting value at the intersection between different market contexts. In the following sections, I will firstly provide some historical context of Valve, the owner of Steam, and situate the Steam platform within the wider game market. After this, I will address how the Steam platform differs from other platforms and why this makes it an interesting case of 'tangled markets'. I will use the key differences between *Counter-Strike: Global Offensive* and *Fortnite* to exemplify how this specific business model cuts across the game design, the platform, and economic practices beyond the platform (Thorhauge and Nielsen, 2021). Finally, I will briefly present the individual chapters of this analysis and their primary findings.

Valve Corporation: incumbent or challenger?

Valve was founded in 1996 by Gabe Logan Newell and Mike Harrington. Both were former employees of Microsoft and Valve's headquarters were physically located relatively close to the corporate headquarters of Microsoft in Redmond, Washington.[1] At the outset, the company primarily focused on game development, and its first title, *Half-Life*, was a considerable commercial success.[2] Mike Harrington left the company in

2000, however, and Gabe Newell took it in new directions. In 2003, the company reincorporated as Valve Corporation, moved its headquarters to Bellevue, Washington, and launched Steam as a game distribution platform. The development throughout the following two decades can be described as a gradual change of emphasis from game development to game services, involving the software and hardware solutions that undergird games. In addition to the Steam platform, these include the Steam Machine, the corporation's own series of gaming computers, VR headsets, and Steam Deck, a portable game system running on SteamOS. Even though none of these inventions have shown to be even slightly as successful as the Steam platform, they speak to an ambition that goes beyond game development and into the development and control of the technologies on which games run. Gabe Newell himself ostensibly looks towards Nintendo, one of the core console owners mentioned in Chapter 2, and how this company has used the combined development of games and hardware to push innovation within the domain of gaming.[3] He is also reported to have launched harsh critiques of the processes of console game development and the proprietary strategies employed by Microsoft and Apple,[4] announcing open-source development as the future of gaming.[5] Valve still develops new game titles such as *Artifact* (2018) and releases new titles in established Valve-owned franchises, such as *Half-Life: Alyx* for VR. Yet, as Boluk and LeMieux note, the business strategy of Valve is to a lesser degree the development of original IP and to a larger degree the monetization of the metagame (2017), and the flagship game titles currently driving the bulk of player numbers on the platform, such as *Counter-Strike: Global Offensive, Dota 2*, and *Team Fortress 2* (see Chapter 7) have emerged from modding communities (Kücklich, 2005; Postigo, 2007; Joseph, 2018) and have later been acquired by Valve (Boluk and Lemieux, 2017).

According to available sources, Valve earns the majority of its revenue from Steam controlling 50–70 per cent of the PC game market[6]; however, it is difficult to obtain any updated data on this. As a private company seated in Bellevue, Washington, Valve is not legally obligated to publish financial statements that allow for a comparison with other market actors in this business segment and in the market of digital games as a whole, and in this way, no systematic accounts of the company's and the platform's earnings are available, except for online game journalism (Kotaku, PC Gamer, GameSpot, and so on) and documents published in relation to various lawsuits (Valve Corporation verus Activision Blizzard Inc.; Australian Federal Court versus Valve). In an interview with *Forbes* in 2011, Gabe Newell said that Valve per employee (250 at the time) was more profitable than Google and Apple.[7] According to the same magazine, Newell today owns about one quarter of the company and his net worth is $3.9 billion.[8] The Steam platform allegedly made $4.3 billion in 2017, but microtransactions do not seem to be part of that number.[9]

In Kerr's overview of business segments in the contemporary market of digital games (Kerr, 2017: 40; see Chapter 2), Steam appears as an intermediary in the segment of core computer games, with no further explanation. It has been the primary intermediary within this business segment for more than a decade, but it is difficult to find any robust data that can qualify this point further. When Kerr does not spend many words on Steam or Valve in her account, it is very likely due to the lack of publicly available documents about the company. Nevertheless, it is fair to say that Steam has been a key intermediary in the segment of PC gaming for more than a decade, and to many, the platform is synonymous with PC gaming. Other platforms have carved out their own niches within this business segment, such as Itch.io and gog.com, and large market actors continuously challenge Steam's position, such as EA's Origin and Epic game store. EA launched Origin and withdrew its games from Steam in 2011 in an attempt to challenge Steam's position as a primary storefront but did not manage to attract enough users, and in 2019, EA's game titles reappeared on the Steam platform.[10] More recently, Epic has harnessed the immense popularity of *Fortnite* to leverage its own store in direct competition with Steam. As I will return to in Chapter 7, this implies that Epic's own games are not available on the Steam platform, along with another group of game titles from game publishers that have made exclusive deals with the company. One of Epic's primary competition parameters is that it takes a smaller share of game sales,[11] in this way presenting a better deal to third-party developers and publishers, and time will tell if this strategy is enough to arm-wrestle Steam. At the time of writing, Microsoft's acquisition of Activision Blizzard[12] and the expansion of its PC game pass across a wider geographical area may pose another threat to Steam's status within the segment of PC gaming.

Thus, in Fligstein's terminology (Fligstein, 2001; see Chapter 3), Steam can be defined as a challenger in the wider game market and an incumbent in the market of PC gaming. While the large game console owners – Sony, Nintendo, and Microsoft – hold the position of incumbents in the segment of console games, the core of the old market, Steam has historically been the 'opposition leader', with its strong position in the somewhat alternative market of PC games. Certainly, this pattern is not as stable as is somewhat implied in Fligstein's theory of markets as fields. Kerr mentions diversification inside as well as from outside the game market as two important tendencies in the contemporary market (2017), including incumbents' attempts to consolidate their market position through acquisitions and large tech companies entering the scene. Microsoft's recent acquisition of Activision Blizzard can be seen as a reflection of the first tendency, while Apple's, Google's, and Tencent's positions as the largest actors in the wider game market (Kerr, 2017) can be seen as a reflection of the second. In this way, it is very likely that we will see the current market order change towards a higher concentration dominated by actors from outside the game market in the future. Nevertheless, Valve has managed to retain its primary position in the domain of PC games despite Epic's strong attempts (and endless money supply) to challenge this position, and Microsoft and Sony releasing first-party game titles such as *Halo Infinite* and *Horizon Zero Dawn* on the Steam platform indicates that they have accepted the Steam platform as a market standard in this domain.

Notably, this battle is fought at the level of storefronts. As I point out in Chapter 2, traditional game consoles are proprietary technologies for executing game code with a focus on content curation, and the incumbents controlling these game consoles have effectively used this power to maintain a market order with a few large actors. The new market actors entering the scene maintain comparably lower entrance barriers as concerns content, while they have effectively integrated and monopolized digital game retail. Thus, neither Google, Apple, nor Tencent are traditional game developers or publishers but rather control major storefronts in the form of Google Play, the App Store, and the Tencent App Store, which are primary entry points to smartphones and tablets. In this way, as always, the quest for market dominance goes through the storefront as a key entry point. It is with this in mind that I will analyse the Steam platform as a tangled market. However, in its current form, the platform is more than a storefront.

Storefront, social network, or tangled market?

As will be addressed in more detail in Chapter 5, the Steam platform was introduced at the Game Developers Conference in 2002, offering players easier access to their games and providing new ways for publishing, billing, managing digital rights, and so on.[13] During its first years, it primarily functioned as a download client for Valve's own game titles, but in 2005, Steam started contracting with third-party publishers[14] and by the beginning of 2007, more than a hundred game titles from Steam and other publishers were available on the platform. At the time of writing, the Steam platform features more than 58,000 unique game titles and mods, of which approximately 13,000 are played by at least one player. According to Valve's own home page, the total number of players fluctuates around 20 million.[15] On the basis of these numbers, it is fair to say that Steam has succeeded as a multi-sided market connecting game publishers and as a key intermediator in the business segment of core computer games. However, during this historical process, it has developed into more than a storefront. The Steam platform obviously includes a range of gaming services, such as matchmaking and leader boards, to support multiplayer gaming. On top of this comes another range of social features, including achievement badges, trading cards, and review and news systems, which are not available to the same extent on competing platforms. Werning defines the platform as a 'de facto social network' (2019) due to the way it enables user interaction beyond the contexts of individual game titles. Indeed, one of the Steam platform's primary assets is its highly dedicated community that participates actively in platform events such as sales (Werning, 2019) and tournaments (Zanescu et al, 2020).

Werning states that Steam's platformization strategy is 'built on games and the pervasiveness of play in contemporary society ... rather than monetizing the connectedness of information ... or people' (2019: 105). In the subsequent chapters, however, I will address how Steam is definitely monetizing the connectedness of information and people. I will argue that the core of Steam's business models lies at the intersection between player communities and market relations through transactions on the platform. I will analyse how Valve has expanded the original game store with a range of contexts for economic exchange that transform community interaction into market interactions by way of the platform features. This market logic cuts across game design, platform features, and wider economic practices in ways that do not fit neatly into established business models such as initial point of sale, subscription, advertising, or upselling. Instead, it is based on the economic actions of the gamers beyond the game within different contexts of economic exchange on and beyond the platform.

For instance, Rune Nielsen and I compare the business models of *Fortnite* and *Counter-Strike: Global Offensive* and the way skins are part of the two platforms' business rationales (Thorhauge and Nielsen, 2021). While the business models of both games revolve around skins, that is, cosmetic items that do not involve any gameplay advantage (see Chapter 5), they do this in very different ways that reflect the more general business rationales of the platforms. In *Fortnite*, which is published by Epic and available in its game store, skins are obtained through battle passes or the in-game store. Their prices are set by the designer, and considerable effort has been put into designing distinctions and cooperating with partner brands such as Marvel to make skins attractive and worth the price put on them, from 500 to 2,000 'V-Bucks' or 5–20 dollars. Thus, skins are relatively high-priced in *Fortnite* as compared to *Counter-Strike: Global Offensive*, which is published by Valve and available on the Steam platform. In *Counter-Strike: Global Offensive*, skins are obtained through drops and loot boxes, and do not cost anything at the outset. However, to be able to open a loot box, the player must buy a key for 1–2 dollars. Once a player unlocks a skin, it will appear in their inventory independently of the game and be tradable in the Steam community market, where prices fluctuate considerably more. Since all economic transactions on the platform pass through the Steam Wallet, giving Steam a share, the platform earns its revenue not at the initial point of sale but in the subsequent economic actions performed by players on and beyond it. Thus, the 'skin economies' of *Fortnite* and *Counter-Strike: Global Offensive* vary considerably and reflect the general business strategies of platforms: Epic's storefront and Steam's tangled market. While the *Fortnite* business model can be defined as an aggressive upselling strategy employed within the context of the game, the *Counter-Strike: Global Offensive* one can be defined as a market strategy employed within the wider contexts of the Steam platform as a market context and generally reflects Valve's double position as game publisher and platform owner with regard to this particular game title.

Accordingly, the aim of the four subsequent chapters is to address in more detail how the historical development of the Steam platform, its current design, the way different market actors transform this platform design into business strategies, and the economic practices emerging beyond the platform all shed light on the characteristics of the Steam business model as compared to other platform business models. One key point of my analysis is that the Steam platform cannot be analysed and interpreted independently of the wider historical and economic context within which it is situated. For instance, the historical development of the platform should be interpreted as an outcome of interactions and negotiations between key groups on the platform and how this has been handled by the platform owner (Burgess, 2021). Moreover, one thing is the possible intentions behind the platform design; another is the particular way different groups of actors cluster around different aspects of the platform's functionalities or 'environment of expected use' (Light et al, 2018) shaping what can be defined as a 'local market order'. In this way, the analysis also reflects how a platform study grounded in an economic-sociological notion of markets and market orders allows for an empirically grounded investigation of patterns of platform use.

To conduct this analysis, I have collected a range of data focusing on Steam's development over time, the platform's current affordances, the way different market actors transform these affordances into business strategies, and how the economic practices on the platform extend beyond it. In order to map Steam's development over time, I have collected all Steam blog updates and news about platform changes, categorized these with regard to the business emphasis they reflect, and organized them in a timeline. Since the current Steam client only goes back to 2010, I have used The Wayback Machine[16] to collect news back to 2003. In order to map the market affordances of the platform in its current form, I have identified all sections of the Steamworks documentation that concern economic transactions and used these to map the different contexts of economic exchange on the Steam platform and how they relate. In order to map how these affordances are actually being used by different economic actors on the platform, I have collected available application programming interface (API) data on all game titles and mods with regard to their year of release, publisher, and price in the game store, and combined these with available API data with regard to the number of players at the time of data collection. Moreover, I have collected data from the Steam platform interface to assess actors' relative presence in the Steam community workshop and market as alternative contexts of economic exchange. Finally, I have collected a sample of third-party websites that utilize the Steam platform in a number of ways, in order to categorize the uses and discuss how they play into the Steam platform economy. I have developed my own scripts in RStudio for these purposes.

In Chapter 5, I will conduct a diachronic affordance analysis (Werning, 2019) of the way the Steam platform has developed from a storefront into various contexts of economic exchange. I will interpret this as a continuous expansion of the scope of economic transactions, and I will suggest that this can be interpreted as a strategic 'disembedment' (see Chapter 3) of player-driven economies into actual market transactions. In Chapter 6, I will map Steam's current platform features, as these can be deducted from the Steamworks documentation offering a range of platform services to third-party developers. My focus will be on the numerous ways in which the platform enables economic transactions, and I will identify the Steam Wallet as the core feature across the Steam storefront, the community market, and the community workshop, which engenders the business model of the Steam platform. In Chapter 7, I will map how different actors on the platform transform these features into actual business strategies. I will describe different actors' emphases on initial point of sale and upselling respectively, and will track their relative presence in the Steam community market and community workshop. On the basis of this analysis, I conclude that large publishers combine initial point of sale and upselling, and smaller publishers stick to initial point of sale, while Valve itself places its primary focus on upselling as well as an overwhelming presence in the Steam community workshop and community market. This indicates that the platform owner has put its primary business emphasis on player trading, while other publishers primarily use the platform as a storefront or a way to access player communities. Finally, in Chapter 8, I address how the economic activities extend beyond the platform on to various third-party trading and gambling sites. I discuss the way game items are transformed into goods, prices, and tokens in these contexts, and how this increases the convertibility of these items and their status as a form of payment. I look at the ways in which Valve, even if it does not earn a share of these transactions, still may have an interest in enabling such economic practices as a way of growing the entire platform economy and consolidating Steam as a general means of payment.

5

Steam's Business Model

In this chapter, I will describe and discuss the gradual development of the Steam platform's business model from a classic retail or multi-sided market to distinct ways of monetizing user participation that set it apart from other platforms. Gaming platforms such as PlayStation Store, Xbox Market, and Epic Games Store rely primarily on retail, and major media platforms such as YouTube rest on a relatively classic advertisement-based business model, where content is offered to users and advertisement space is sold to advertisers (Caraway, 2011). The primary difference between these platforms and traditional commercial media is the extensive collection of user data that enables a more granulated analysis and classification of user segments (Fourcade and Healy, 2017; Van Dijck et al, 2018) and the scope of commodification (Ørmen and Gregersen, 2022). Steam, on the contrary, denounces advertising as a way of monetizing games on the platform. That is, the platform does not offer a system for integrating ads with content as a way of monetizing users like the one featured by YouTube (see Ørmen and Gregersen, 2022) or the App Store, and the active participation of players on the platform is monetized in ways that differ considerably from the advertisement business model. On the one hand, passive and active player contributions are used to augment and further the effectiveness of the Steam store, that is, to offer 'value-added services' (Jöckel et al, 2008) on the platform. On the other hand, the scope of economic transactions is extended to turn players' economic action into a source of revenue in addition to retail.

In this chapter, I will describe the way Steam's business model has developed throughout the platform's lifetime and argue that the monetization of its social connectedness is based on shaping and reorganizing social interactions as market interactions. That is, by 'disembedding' players' economic action from the player-driven economies and gaming communities in which they originate, and reorganizing them as market interactions, the Steam platform converts the affective value players generate through their gameplay into market value that can be exchanged and put to use elsewhere. In the following, I will firstly provide a little more context of the Steam platform. After this, I will revisit the concept of embeddedness of economic action put forward in Chapter 3 and introduce the concepts of affective value and affective economies. Then, I will conduct a 'diachronic affordance analysis' (Werning, 2019) of Steam's development over time and discuss how the addition and discontinuation of features can be interpreted as expressions of varying business emphases: from retail over monetization of playbour to monetization of player-driven economies. As an extension of this historical overview, I will discuss in more detail how the extended scope of economic transactions on the platform can be described as a 'disembedding' of players' economic action in games and a conversion of affective value into market value.

The Steam platform

Steam was announced by Valve at the international Game Developers Conference in San Jose in March 2002. In the press release for the event, it was described as 'a broadband business platform for direct software delivery and content management allowing users to purchase and start their applications faster than if they install them from a CD'. The press release also pointed out the advantages for developers who were given 'integrated tools for direct content publishing, flexible billing, ensured version control, anti-piracy, and more'.[1] In this way, Valve presented the platform as an offering for players and developers alike, giving the former easier access to their games and the latter a new way of distributing, billing, and updating their games. Accordingly, Steam was, at the outset, conceived as a multi-sided market or 'matchmaker' (Evans and Schmalensee, 2016) connecting game developers and gamer communities. The continuous development of the platform and the ongoing addition and discontinuation of features can be interpreted as a trade-off between the interests of these groups. During its early years, the platform primarily managed to fulfil its offering for gamer communities, featuring Valve's own game titles such as *Half-Life* (1998) and *Counter-Strike* (2000) to an audience of dedicated gamers. However, from 2005, Valve managed to attract more external developers and publishers to the platform. By the beginning of 2007, the platform featured more than a hundred game titles from various publishers and Valve was turning into a multi-sided market. Today, Steam features more than 58,000 unique games and mods, as observed from API data. A majority of these are very likely small projects published by hobbyists or 'modders'. As I will get back to in Chapter 7, about 13,000 of these games are played by at least one player, and a few large game titles on the platform draw the bulk of player numbers. Nevertheless, according to available sources, the

Steam platform dominates the market of PC games and represents the 'de facto PC gaming platform',[2] only recently challenged by the Epic Games Store and the Microsoft Game Pass. It offers a broad range of additional features on top of the original software delivery and content management functionalities, including the Steam community workshop, where players can create items for games, the Steam community market, where players can trade items from games, trading cards, which can be collected and traded in the market, the Points Shop, where players can buy 'vanity items' for experience points earned in specific games, and so on.

This course of development has been described as a 'disruptive platformization strategy', with constant feature changes challenging established business models in game companies and social media (Werning, 2019). Valve's business model is no longer based on creating original IP (if it ever was), but rather on 'colonising, expropriating, and assimilating metagames into a framework of benevolent capitalism' (Boluk and LeMieux, 2017: 261). Boluk and LeMieux define 'metagames' as 'those external rules or social customs built in, around, and through videogames' (2017: 228). This includes players' active conversations, contributions, and competitions in relation to specific game titles, that is, everything that cannot be packaged and sold. Steam's unceasing feature changes can be interpreted as a continuous exploration and exploitation of such metagames as an alternative revenue model alongside its retail market. Moreover, the platform effectively allows these metagames to extend on to various third-party websites (Zanescu et al, 2020, 2021; Thorhauge and Nielsen, 2021), which somewhat resonates with the ways major platforms have strategically designed their APIs to 'platformize the web' (Helmond, 2015). With this concept, Helmond points to the ways in which platforms decentralize their features (for example, the Facebook 'like button') across the internet and recentralize platform-ready data (for example, 'like data') as an extension of this. This process of decentralization/recentralization serves the purposes of an advertisement-based revenue model where ever more granular user data informs the creation of user segments that can be sold to advertisers. In the case of Steam and its alternative business emphasis on markets and transactions, however, the strategy of the Steam API concerns the expansion of market interactions and economic transactions on and beyond the platform. Indeed, as I will return to in Chapter 8, the third-party websites that enable trading and gambling with items from Steam-based games extend economic practices beyond the context of the platform, while the platform remains the primary 'transaction mechanism' in these economic practices. Before I turn to these economic practices, however, I will address how the platform, by way of its key features, enables and shapes its market interaction and converts the affective value of gamer communities into market value in the process. To make this argument, I will return to the notion of economic embeddedness explained in Chapter 3 and introduce the concept of affective value in addition to this.

The conversion of affective value into market value

In Chapter 3, I presented the concept of embeddedness and how it has been addressed differently in the context of economic sociology. In Polanyi's (1944) use of the term, embeddedness refers to a general historical transformation where markets and market interactions gain increased importance in society. Economic interactions may be embedded in and thus guided by social structures of groups and communities, or they may be disembedded from these social structures operating in accordance with their own logics, the latter being the case in market societies. In comparison, Granovetter (1985) takes a more literal network-analytical approach to the concept, pointing to the fact that economic actors are in practice social actors who are embedded in social networks that influence their economic action. Later works somewhat attempt to reconcile these differences by referring to a 'soft' Granovetter and a 'hard' Polanyi (Peck, 2013; Tubaro, 2021), while others point out that these are essentially different approaches: while Polanyi represents a political-economic perspective, Granovetter represents an organizational and network-analytical viewpoint (Krippner and Alvarez, 2007). The concept has been applied to the context of digital media in terms of the potential 'disembeddedness' or 'deep embeddedness' of online labour (Tubaro, 2021), but it has not, to my knowledge, been applied in the field of game studies. In this chapter, I will demonstrate how both approaches to the concept of embeddedness represent useful frameworks for discussing the specific ways in which the Steam platform strategically reorganizes player interaction as market interaction through the integration of transactional affordances (Manzerolle and Daubs, 2021) across the platform. I will argue that this reorganization of economic action from a 'Polanyian' perspective can be defined as a 'disembedment' of economic interaction from those player communities in which they originate. From a 'Granovettarian' perspective, I will argue that this disembedment of economic action is not absolute, as Polanyi also points out, albeit for other reasons. Users on the Steam platform are simultaneously gameplayers and market actors, and their economic decisions, such as their assessment of goods and prices in the Steam community market, are rooted in the norms and values shared among communities of gamers (Granovetter, 2017: 26). When Granovetter refers to 'norms and values' in this context, he most likely refers to the definition of these terms as they are applied in the context of sociology. For the sake of the forthcoming analysis, I will expand these terms, applying the concept of affective value as it has been developed in the contexts of marketing theory and Marxist feminism.

At first glance, brand marketing and Marxist feminism do not have a lot in common. However, within both fields of research, the affects and emotions shared by consumers and platform users are foregrounded as a key source of the value that makes up large brands and forms the core of platform business models. Henry Jenkins (2006), for instance, identifies 'affective economics' as a marketing trend focusing on 'the emotional underpinnings of consumer decision making' due to the need 'to quantify desire, to measure connections, to commodify commitments [and] to transform all of the above into return of investment (2006: 61–2). This approach to marketing, according to Jenkins, involves the strategic expansion of consumers' empirical, social, and intellectual investment to shape consumption patterns (2006: 63). Indeed, according to Adam Arvidsson, brand value rests on 'a socialised production process in which consumers create symbolic and affective wealth around brands in their everyday communicative interaction' (Arvidsson, 2006: 188). While Arvidsson's analysis involves a Marxist critique of brand value and brand ownership, Jenkins maintains that this marketing trend has positive as well as negative implications. It allows advertisers to direct collective intelligence towards their own ends, but it also allows consumers to form their own collective bargaining structure (Jenkins, 2006: 63). He does address the exploitative aspects of this, and Marc Andrejevic contends that marketers may in fact have something different in mind, 'not a grass-roots formation with a range of ties to other community members, but dispersed individuals who can be engaged and enlisted for the purpose of brand management' (Andrejevic, 2011: 615). This ambiguity of affective value is also foregrounded in Marxist feminist research, yet from a slightly different perspective. This field of research connects the notion of affective value with general feminist critiques of domestic work as unpaid labour in capitalist economies (Fortunati, 1995). Kylie Jarett rhetorically labels platform users 'digital housewifes' and their activities on Twitter, Pinterest, and Instagram as exploited labour (2016). She draws, among other things, on the 'affective turn' in media studies, addressing the 'ebb and flow of relational intensities in our digitally mediated interactions (2016: 113), but adds to this strand of research important considerations of the way they are actively exploited in the context of commercial digital media. That is, the 'generation of affective intensities is … integral not only to what we do as users on the site, but also to the economic model of the digital media industry' (2016: 118). Her key example to illustrate this relationship is a Facebook story recounting how the first thing a woman does upon hearing about her cancer diagnosis is write a status update on Facebook to tell everyone she knows (2016: 114). This piece of communication is an emotionally meaningful act as this woman reaches out to her social network for support, while it serves, in the context of Facebook, as a vehicle for advertising too. The Facebook stories page abounds with such emotionally intense stories that serve to increase traffic towards the advertisements that form the core of its business model.

The 'ebb and flow of relational intensities' is present in the context of gaming as well. Key components of the gameplay experience, such as competition, immersion, and role play, thrive on and amplify players' affection towards the games and the items and characters they contain. Yet, while it seems straightforward that affective intensities increase attention and traffic in advertisement-based platform business models, the Steam platform model is not based on advertising. Instead, I will argue, players' affective intensities are vital in creating the value that is exchanged through market interactions on and beyond the platform. In this way, the reorganization of platform interactions into market interactions through a process of 'disembedment', in Polanyi's definition of the term, can also be interpreted as a conversion of 'relational intensities' or affective value residing in gaming communities into market value that can be exchanged and leveraged elsewhere. In the remaining sections of this chapter, I will substantiate this line of thought through an analysis of the Steam platform's historical development and the changing business emphases this reflects. As an extension of this, I will discuss how this change of emphasis from retail to player-driven economies can be interpreted as a strategic monetization of affective value generated in gaming communities.

A diachronic accordance analysis of the Steam platform's development

In his analysis of Steam as a social medium, Werning (2019) addresses the platform's development over time. He emphasizes the importance of a 'diachronic' perspective to pinpoint general patterns of development in the histories of platforms as a way of understanding on their contemporary form. He combines data from tech blogs as well as feature updates on the platform and uses this to trace two major patterns of change: the adoption of elements that make the use of Steam playful in itself, and the transformation of Steam into a 'de facto social network' (2019: 110). In this chapter, I will take a similar approach, though I will focus on the way player contributions in the form of communicative and economic action are directly integrated into the platform business model. My focus will be on the changing business emphases of the Steam platform, and the strategic advance of player-driven economies over time. For this purpose, I have found the Steam blog and press releases to be particularly informative, partly because they mark what can be considered major changes in the history of the platform, and partly because the 'corporate rhetoric' accompanying these updates may yield some insights into the strategies behind the changes. Accordingly, I have collected and categorized the Steam blog updates and press releases available on the platform and organized these on a timeline along with their content. Since the Steam blog was introduced in 2010, and data on the platform only dates to this year, I have collected the news sections from snapshots available on the Wayback Machine, extending the timeline back to 2005. In the following, I will briefly summarize the historical development of the Steam platform. After this, I will discuss three major business emphases reflected in the continuous addition and discontinuation of features on the Steam platform: the development of the steam store, the monetization of playbour (Kücklich, 2005), and the extended scope of economic transactions.

From download client to tangled market

As mentioned in the introduction, the Steam platform was launched as an offering for publishers and players alike, giving players easier access to their games and publishers more flexible tools for digital content management and distribution. This initial focus on the platform as a multi-sided market was soon supplemented with a range of alternative approaches to monetizing user-generated content and expanding the scope of economic transactions across the platform. Moreover, the platform's development over time indicates an ongoing trade-off between the primary user groups: publishers and users.

During its first years, public statements about Steam's development primarily relate to the arrival of new publishers and game titles, such as Sega and Sony making their games available on the platform. These statements continue to appear throughout the platform's historical development, indicating the importance of strategic alliances with other publishers and platform owners as key to the platform's success as a market for PC games. In the same period, a few features are added that indicate Steam's business emphasis at the time: the 'Steamworks development kit' in 2008, offering 'PC game developers and publishers access to the game features and services available through Steam,[3] the introduction of 'source mods' the same year, addressing the modding communities, and in-game DLC in 2009, a first step towards alternative ways of monetizing games on the platform.

In 2010, Valve introduces a new client for the platform and extends its services to Mac, and in the following few years, several important features are added that indicate how Steam uses the growing community to extend and refine the features of the game store, while introducing several features indicating new business emphases beyond it. As concerns the first, the introduction of personal recommendations in 2011, the Steam Greenlight Initiative in 2012, and Steam reviews in 2013 all relate to the continuous development of the Steam store, offering recommendations based on the increased availability of user data and integrating active player contributions in the evaluation and selection of game titles available. At the same time, the introduction of the Steam Wallet and the Steam community market in 2012 and paid mods in the Steam workshop in 2015 indicate the development of an alternative business emphasis based on player-driven economies. Later developments also bear witness to the limitation of these business emphases, such as the replacement of the Greenlight Initiative with Steam Direct in 2017, discontinuing the system that allowed Steam users to vote for specific game titles, and the attempt to handle the strong controversy following the introduction of economic transactions in the Steam workshop. In the following, I will dive deeper into the different types of business emphases this indicates: the continuous expansion of the Steam store, the monetization of playbour (Kücklich, 2005), and the expanded scope of economic transactions.

The continuous expansion of the Steam store

Steam was introduced as a tool for direct content publishing and flexible billing, offering a new digital outlet for publishers in the game market. This reflects a general course of development in the game industry throughout the 2000s from physical retail to digital publishing (Kerr, 2017). In this way, a core business emphasis at the platform's beginning and throughout its development has been the Steam store, where a diverse group of publishers can sell their games to Steam users, with Steam earning a share of each transaction in the same manner as other extended market places (Doyle, 2013) or market platforms such as Google Play and the App Store. Indeed, this aspect of the Steam platform corresponds perfectly with Evans and Schmalensee's notion of multi-sided market (2016; see Chapter 3).

This business emphasis is reflected in the 'corporate rhetoric' of Steam press releases and the official Steam blog in several ways. Most notably, it can be detected in the recurring news about key publishers or key game titles arriving for the platform, boosting its relative value as a market for PC game titles. Moreover, several features added throughout this historical development also indicate how the platform has been expanded and amended to support this business emphasis. For instance, the release of the Steamworks development kit in 2008 helps developers and publishers make their games available on Steam. Unlike the source engine, Valve's original game engine, which is licensed for commercial actors, the Steamworks development kit is offered free of charge, underlining that the business models are not to license proprietary software but to attract a critical mass of publishers. While the Steamworks development kit in this way aims to ease the lives of publishers, another group of features reflect Steam's active integration of users and user data, their 'value-added services' (Jöckel et al, 2008). With the growing number of users and the resultant amount of user data, Steam can announce the introduction of personalized recommendations in 2011, while the 2013 introduction of user reviews integrates more active player contributions on the platform. Also, the different ways of activating and involving Steam users can be detected in the numerous seasonal sale events celebrated on the Steam blog, in the platform interface, and by active users in a sort of recurrent 'community ritual' (Werning, 2019).

However, several developments also indicate the conflicting interests between the key actors involved in this business model: the publishers and the gamers. Thus, the Greenlight programme is introduced in 2012 to enlist 'the community's help in selecting some of the next games to be released on Steam'.[4] This can be interpreted as another way of integrating active user contributions in the curation of content on the platform, while it also comes with a few built-in obstacles, such as developers having to campaign their games before they are even developed. Accordingly, the programme was replaced with Steam Direct in 2017, removing user votes as a key threshold to accessing the platform. The change was explained with the wish to 'remove the barrier between developers and their audience',[5] while a franker interpretation is that the programme yielded users too much power over publishers. Similarly, the collective attempts by users to decide the future of specific game titles through 'review bombing', also reflected in the Steam blog posts, indicates how the Steam platform aims to attract a critical mass of developers and gamers alike to sustain its market, while it has to handle conflicting interests between these key groups, presenting itself 'strategically to each of these audiences, carving out a role and a set of expectations that is acceptable to each and also serves its own financial interests, while resolving or at least eliding the contradictions between them' (Gillespie, 2010: 353). In this way, Steam's development over time can be interpreted as an attempt at attracting a critical mass of publishers and users to sustain its market and to integrate players' passive and active contributions in its value-added services (Jöckel et al, 2008). On certain occasions, these two business groups conflict, leading to controversies and changes in the platform features and user interface.

The monetization of playbour

One key to the Steam platform's success as a market for PC gaming is its integration of active player contributions in the continuous expansion and refinement of the game store (Jöckel et al, 2008; Werning, 2019). However, player contributions are not limited to user data, forum posts, and reviews. The 'modding community' has represented a distinct and important user-group throughout the platform's entire history. Indeed, the platform was introduced as a download client for the initial *Counter-Strike*, which was itself a 'mod'. Moreover Source, the game engine in which *Counter-Strike* was created, was from the beginning made freely available to modders, while licensed to commercial actors (Kerr, 2017). Modding refers to the activity of modifying games. These modifications can range from minor changes or add-ons to total conversions, with the former being more common than the latter (Postigo, 2007). It is often organized in communities that represent one distinct practice in 'participatory culture' (Jenkins, 2006), an idealistic and co-creative approach where fans are seen as 'produsers' (Bruns, 2008), actively modifying and elaborating on the universes they admire. While this is often approached in positive terms as an empowerment of individual media users, active contributions made in this way also represent a major source of profit for diverse platforms (Banks, 2013) and a form of free labour (Terranova, 2000). For this reason, critical approaches to the phenomenon address the uneasy relationship between the idealized non-capitalistic nature of modding and the diverse ways in which these contributions are commercially appropriated (Kücklich, 2005; Banks, 2013; Joseph, 2018), often through the terms and conditions and end user licence agreements of game engines and other development tools.

In terms of the Steam platform, the integration of active player contributions takes several forms, ranging from the analysis of user data for personalized recommendations over the enabling of forums and user reviews to the Steam community workshop, where players can create additional content for game titles that make of this feature. The addition of specific features throughout the platform's history bears witness to the way this business emphasis has evolved from the launch of the Steam community (2007), reviews (2013), and the gradual expansion of the workshop, to the introduction of economic transactions in this workshop (2015), which turned out to be quite controversial (Joseph, 2018). These features were introduced with *The Elder Scrolls V: Skyrim* as a pilot due to its highly committed modding community. Now modders would be able to sell their creations earning a 25 per cent share of the revenue (with Steam earning 30 per cent and publisher Bethesda Software earning another 45 per cent) (Joseph, 2018: 691). While this feature change was introduced as an ambition to give 'community mod makers the opportunity to earn money doing what they love',[6] it was received quite differently in the modding community, where it was interpreted as a commodification of modding as a hobby. Eventually, Bethesda Software had to remove the feature and post an excuse, and the feature was limited to Valve-published games for a while. With reference to Harvey's concept of 'accumulation by dispossession' (Harvey, 2005), Joseph describes this course of events as a case of 'digital dispossession' where the assumed public goods of modding communities are dispossessed by Valve. He points out that the controversy 'brought to the forefront a series of social contradictions that had previously been latent in the practice of modding' (2018: 704), that is, the understanding of modding as a non-capitalist endeavour versus the strong links between the modding communities and the game industry. Nevertheless, several game titles today make use of this feature, in practice allowing players to sell items they create for money, sharing the revenues with the publisher and the platform owner. In some cases, this also involves a process of curation where the publisher evaluates the quality of the items in question. Even though this is only the case with a tiny number of game titles as compared to the total number of titles available on the platform, several of these are highly profiled on the platform, as measured in player numbers, and they are published by Valve (see Chapter 7). However, as regards the uneasy relationship between voluntary contributions and commodification, this conflict is dissolved in the context of the Steam community market, where active player contributions are identical to their economic action.

Expanding the scope of economic transactions

The monetization of playbour explained in the previous section involves one important step away from the classic retail market as envisioned in the original press release. However, the integration of transactional affordances (Manzerolle and Daubs, 2021) across a range of contexts on the platform implies another step away from this business strategy, going from an indirect incorporation of playbour as part of Steam's 'value-added services' (Jöckel et al, 2008) to a direct incorporation by way of taxation. The introduction of the Steam community market (2013) and economic transactions in the Steam workshop (2015) are both indications of this. Whenever a player creates an item and puts it on sale in the Steam community workshop, money earned from potential sales will be stored in his or her Steam Wallet. And whenever a player unlocks or earns a 'marketable item' in a game title that has enabled this feature, they will be able to list it in the Steam community market, and money earned from potential sales will be stored in his or her Steam Wallet. Needless to say, Valve earns a share of all of these transactions, turning the growing number of economic transactions into an alternative source of revenue. Valve's own flagship titles on the Steam platform, *Team Fortress 2* (2007), *Counter-Strike: Global Offensive* (2012), and *Dota 2* (2013), seem to build their revenue primarily on this business logic (see Chapter 7), differing considerably from the business logic of the classic retail market.

While the introduction of economic transactions in the Steam community workshop, as described in the previous section, spawned a great deal of controversy, the introduction of the Steam community market, trade offers, and trading cards in 2013 did not ignite any fires. This may be due to these activities being somewhat more of an extension of well-known economic practices in games moving from the level of games and game communities to the level of the platform. Thus, the reorganization of economic action in games into actual market interaction seemed minor due to the immediate resemblances between the activities in question, such as trading cards, exchanging items, and bargaining in the process. Nevertheless, in the wider contexts of the platform economy, this reorganization is profound, creating a direct link between the non-market economic interaction of game economies and communities and the business model of the Steam platform, and dissolving the contradictions between the modding communities and invested commercial interests in the process, 'turning prosumption into a capitalist endeavor per se' (Thorhauge and Nielsen, 2021).

The monetization of player interaction as a process of 'disembedment'

With the Steam platform, Valve has proved particularly apt at monetizing player-driven economies. Of course, several major platforms in the networked era have turned user interaction into a key business model through advertising, but Valve's approach differs considerably from these platforms as it rests on the strategic expansion of economic transactions and the direct incorporation of players' economic action into its business model. In the previous sections, I have described the continuous development of Valve's business emphases on the Steam platform as a gradual development from a classic retail store and multi-sided market to various ways of monetizing user-generated content and users' economic action in the Steam community workshop, the community market, and other contexts of the platform. While the game store most likely represents the key source of revenue, the strategic enabling, shaping, and taxing of players' economic interaction are seemingly the most important sources of income for Valve's own flagship game titles on the platform (see Chapter 7). According to Werning, this platform business model is based on 'the pervasiveness of play in contemporary society rather than monetizing the connectedness of information (Via Google's search algorithms) or people (via Facebook's social graph) online' (Werning, 2019: 105). However, Steam definitely monetizes the connectedness of information and people, albeit in a way that differs considerably from other platforms. It converts affective value into market value through the 'disembedment' or reorganization of interaction in game economies and gaming communities into market interactions.

In my introduction to the concept of embeddedness (see also Chapter 3), I point out that it can be interpreted at several levels. In Polanyi's political-economic account of the concept, embeddedness refers to the historical process in which market interactions are 'disembedded' from social structures and market societies emerge. Markets and market interactions did exist in premodern times but were generally subordinated to or 'embedded within' social structures of groups and hierarchies. In market societies, market interactions are 'disembedded' from social structures and function in accordance with their own logics (Polanyi, 1944). Indeed, markets increasingly define the laws for other relationships and processes in society through a process of commodification (see Chapter 9). From this political-economic perspective, the strategic introduction of economic transactions into the Steam community workshop and community market can be interpreted as a 'disembedment' of the economic relationships existing in the economies of games and game communities into market interactions. While the introduction of economic transactions in the form of paid mods may be presented as an innocent attempt to give 'community mod makers the opportunity to earn money doing what they love,[7] it profoundly reorganizes social and economic relationships in the modding communities and transforms them into market relationships, and the items being exchanged, formerly considered to be 'common goods', are now transformed into commodities (Joseph, 2018). That is, while the virtual objects themselves remain unchanged, their status in the process of exchange is profoundly altered and so is the relationship between the platform users as economic agents in the process of exchange. This reorganization of player interaction into market interaction is a first important step in the monetization of player-driven economies. Yet, users' status as market actors on the Steam platform does not necessarily exclude or eliminate their status as game players and members of gaming communities. Indeed, the potential simultaneity of social roles represents another key aspect in the conversion of affective value into market value.

In Granovetter's account of the concept, embeddedness refers to the fact that economic actors are also social actors enmeshed in social contexts that shape their economic actions. Thus, he addresses the level of social networks and the 'norms, values and moral economy' that condition the choices of economic actors (2017: 26). While Granovetter refers to these concepts as they are defined and applied in the context of sociology, I expand the notion of value at the beginning of this chapter to include the affective value that makes up large brands and forms the core of platform economies according to the diverse research fields of brand marketing and Marxist feminism. That is, brands derive their value from symbolic and affective wealth created through communicative interaction (Arvidsson, 2006), and advertisement-based platforms rely on the 'affective intensities' of users to generate the attention and the traffic that drives this business model (Jarett, 2016). In the context of the Steam platform, relational intensities do not generate value through traffic or attention. Relational intensities are an integrated part of the gameplay experience; they form the value players attach to game worlds, fellow players, and outcomes, and one key reason people play games in the first place. At the same time, these values condition the choices of players as economic actors in related market contexts where game items are transformed into goods that are bought and sold at certain prices. Indeed, the varying value attached to items in these markets is rooted directly in the 'norms, values and moral economy' of the game worlds and gaming communities from which they originate.

One of the most salient expressions of this interplay between affective value and market value is the key role of 'skins' in emergent business models in the domain of gaming (see Chapter 2). Until now, I have used the term 'game items' whenever I have referred to the virtual objects that are created in the Steam community workshop or traded in the community market. Yet, most of these belong to a group of game objects labelled 'skins' due to their purely cosmetic function in the game. Skins do not represent any gameplay advantage – they will not make the player run faster or aim better in the game – but they will endow their owner with prestige rooted in the value communities of gamers attach to them. Traditional communities of gamers tend to place great importance on purchasable items being purely cosmetic, and distinguish sharply between this and 'pay-to-win' games where players can buy themselves to progress and victory (Jarett, 2021). That is, they don't seem to have an issue with the commodification of play, as this happens in emergent business models, but rather with the potential corruption of perfect competition, an ideal pervading large parts of traditional game culture. This moral denigration of use value in terms of gameplay and the moral acceptance of affective value as a legitimate reason for purchase make skins a common ground between traditional gaming communities and game publishers with regard to appropriate ways of monetizing gameplay. Indeed, the purely affective value of skins may also be what makes them suitable as assets and units of transaction in contexts of skin trading and skin gambling beyond the Steam platform, as I will return to in Chapter 8. However, the interplay between affective value and market value is not just something that is being explored and played around with in such outlandish contexts of the internet; it forms the core of emergent business models in the domain of gaming. *Counter-Strike: Global Offensive*'s as well as *Fortnite*'s business models, however different (see Chapter 4), both rest on this interplay. No matter if skins are the core of an aggressive upselling scheme, such as the one employed by Epic, or a strategic gamblification and financialization scheme, such as the one employed by Valve, it is the affective value generated in gaming communities that is converted into actual purchases and market value in the business models of both games.

I am not the first to make this observation. In his classical work on fan cultures, Matthew Hills (2003) addresses the position of fans between consumer culture and counter-culture. He points out that the romantic notion of fans as opponents of the industry is one-sided and does not capture sufficiently the complex ways in which they are simultaneously counter-consumers and super-consumers in ways that make them obvious targets of the industry. Fans generate value for the industry, Hills argues, through an ongoing and intense attribution of use value to certain media products and merchandise which affect the exchange value of these products and merchandise: 'Many commodities offered on sale on Ebay should, according to the conventional logic of use- and exchange-value, be almost worthless. However, due to many of them having been intensely subjectively valued by fans, such commodities take on a redefined "exchange-value"' (2003: 10). The meaning and affection fans attach to media products and merchandise is, in this way, translated into market value, and this is one reason why fan cultures are extremely valuable to the industry.

From a somewhat different perspective, Christian Fuchs points out that 'Labour time on commercial social media is the conversion of Bourdieusian social, cultural and symbolic capital into Marxian value and economic capital' (2013: 57). Value and capital are obviously not the same, and Fuchs mainly seems to be addressing advertising: 'The more time a user spends on commercial social media, the more data about her/his interests and activities are available and the more advertisements are presented to her/him' (Fuchs, 2013: 57). Nevertheless, he similarly points that the conversion of one type of value or capital into another is a key perspective on the way platforms monetize social connectivity. Indeed, Gabe Newell himself seems to be quite aware of the complex processes of value generation and transformation on the platform he controls. In his close reading of a presentation Gabe Newell gave at the University of Texas in 2013, Daniel Joseph notices the emphasis Newell puts on value as well as the diverse ways in which he uses it (Joseph, 2017). In this talk, Newell refers to value as something produced by workers and as something players attach to items and to other players 'related to status, and affinity, and hierarchy' (Newell cited in Joseph, 2017: 144). On the basis of this, he contends that his 'job is to maximise productivity of users in creating digital goods and services. The markets will determine what the marginal value added of each of those activities are' (2017: 146). Joseph explains these various uses as an extension of the classic and neoclassic notions of value, that is, as something produced by labour and that consumers are willing to pay for. He argues that Steam provides the tools to monetize this value: 'productivity can only be measured here in terms of dollars and cents ... and Steam is a perfect platform to capture that value' (2017: 150). That is, the Steam platform transforms productive play into market value by way of its market features.

Obviously, these authors are addressing very different concepts of value grounded in as disparate analytical frameworks as classic and neoclassic economies, Marxism, and Bourdieu's capital forms. Moreover, Fuch's and Joseph's notions of labour do not seem to include the intense attribution of value Hills points to; they are rather about time expenditure and content generation respectively. However, all of these authors address the strategic conversion of value embedded in communities and social interaction into value that can be exchanged and leveraged elsewhere. The Steam platform's value extraction rests in this continuous interplay between the assignment of value in the context of player communities and the transformation of this value into market value through economic transactions. While the concept of commodification puts emphasis on the transformation of audiences or players into commodities (Smythe, 1981; Fuchs, 2011; Nieborg, 2016), the concept of 'disembedment' is useful for understanding how this happens through a strategic reorganization of player-driven economies and gaming communities into market interactions, that is, through a process of 'dispossession by disembedment'. I will return to the notion of commodification in Chapter 9, where I engage with the extensive literature on this subject and discuss whether the integration of users as economic actors in the Steam platform economy is sufficiently covered by this concept. Before I do so, I will look deeper into the way market interactions are in practice shaped by Steam's platform features (Chapter 6) and the way different types of economic actors operating on the platform transform these affordances into business strategies (Chapter 7). Moreover, I will analyse users' economic practices beyond the platform as a 'monetary network' (Dodd, 1994) that increases the overall platform economy and transforms Steam's gaming communities into potential 'transactional communities' (Schwartz, 2020; Chapter 8).

6

Shaping Market Interactions on the Steam Platform

In Chapter 2, I introduced the notion of 'platform configurations' to cover the development of game platforms across the previous four decades. I observe that it is not just the game platforms themselves that have changed but also the very concept of 'platform', which has altered its meaning from signifying a computational system to signifying large market actors in Big Tech. Thus, the notion of 'platform configurations' includes the platform as a standardized computing system along with another range of factors that constitute contemporary platforms, such as market orders, ownership structures, and value chains. The specific role of the platform as a standardized computing system varies across these configurations from being primarily development and publishing devices to including storefronts and shaping multi-sided markets. The latter involves that platforms are strategically designed to shape market interactions (Srnicek, 2017) in ways that serve the economic interest of the platform owner. In the current chapter, I will analyse in more detail how this is specifically done by the Steam platform, that is, I will analyse the way the platform's API allows third-party actors to operate on the platform though a critical reading of the documentation. The aim is to map and discuss the ways in which the different contexts of economic exchange are made available as sets of strategic design choices by the platform design, more specifically, through the Steamworks API. The Steam platform design shapes the rules of transaction, one of the basic components of the market institution as defined by Fligstein (Fligstein, 1996, 2001), and the diverse arrays of economic interaction enabled through this design lay the ground for Steam's tangled market (see Chapter 3), that is, complex market contexts containing several interconnected and mutually dependent markets and domains of interaction (see Chapter 3).

Critical analyses of digital platform architectures

The critical analysis of platforms has received a great deal of academic attention during the previous decade and quite a few relevant approaches exist. In her critical history of social media, José van Dijck combines actor network theory and political economy. While the first approach emphasizes 'co-evolving networks of technology and people', the second highlights 'the political-economic context in which informational networks grow into powerful industrial players' (2013: 26–7). Van Dijck points out that the two approaches complement each other since we need a combined focus on pre-existing power structures as well as the way this power is 'executed from technological and computational systems' (Van Dijck, 2013: 26–7). Helmond demonstrates how this technological and computational execution is carried out in practice in her analysis of different platforms' APIs (Helmond, 2015). She puts her emphasis on the 'way platforms enact their programmability to decentralize data production and recentralize data collection' (Gerlitz and Helmond, 2013; Helmond, 2015: 5) and demonstrates how this aspect of the platform can be located to the specific construction of the API.

One key example of an API is the so-called 'widget' that enables the integration of services and functions beyond the platform. Helmond explains how YouTube and the now defunct Myspace introduced such widgets at the beginning of the millennium, but with different aims and scopes. While Myspace's use of widgets was aimed at distributing content within its own network, YouTube's was aimed at distributing content across the web, yielding direct access to the site's database of videos from anywhere on the internet (Helmond, 2015: 7). While this strongly consolidates YouTube's power and reach (and the opposite may be the reason for Myspace's decline), Facebook's API takes it one step further, according to Helmond, by turning this into a two-way data stream. On the one hand, the 'like button' extends Facebook's presence beyond the platform; on the other, every time a user clicks the button, data is collected and sent back to Facebook (Helmond, 2015), in this way extending Facebook's presence and data collection far beyond the boundaries of the platform itself. In my analysis of the Steam platform features, I will similarly put my emphasis on the API and how it yields access to features and data on and beyond the platform as a way of consolidating its position as a key market for PC games. The object of my analysis will be the 'Steamworks API' and the way it grants third-party developers access to the microtransaction system, player data, inventory services, and so on. The strategic design of the Steamworks API does not only concern the production and collection of data (although this certainly plays a role) but also the way economic transactions are shaped and enabled on and beyond the platform, effectively defining the rules of market interactions (Fligstein, 2001; Srnicek, 2017) on Steam as a market context. In the subsequent sections, I will dive deeper into the way market interactions are in practice shaped by the platform design, as this can be deduced from the Steamworks documentation. First, however, I will discuss how this documentation can be analysed and interpreted as an indication of this.

The Steam platform documentation as a rhetorical device

The Steamworks documentation is a voluminous collection of documents explaining to developers and publishers how they can make the most of the Steam platform. It covers a range of textual genres, such as guides, best practices, FAQs, and API references, that delineate what is possible or not possible and what is seen as desirable or undesirable from the perspective of the platform owner. Obviously, it does not reveal every relevant detail about Steam's platform design. As I will return to, certain information is remarkably non-available in the Steamworks documentation, such as Steam's share of transactions in the community market, or the Steam Wallet as a key feature in terms of its earnings. In this way, the documentation and the accompanying API references can be interpreted at more than one level. They can be interpreted as a description of what is possible and what is specifically *not* possible on the platform, that is, the 'rules of product and service development, as well as market interactions ... set by the platform owner' (Srnicek, 2017: 47), or what Fligstein defines as 'the rules of interaction' in markets as fields of strategic action (Fligstein, 2001). They can also be interpreted as an indication of what the platform owner has an interest in promoting and *not* promoting or making available to the public, what Gillespie refers to as the politics of platforms (Gillespie, 2010). From this perspective, the relative emphasis on certain aspects of the system and lack of emphasis on others can give an indication of the more general business strategies of the platform owner. In the subsequent sections, I will use these insights to analyse the way market interactions are shaped on the platform (Srnicek, 2017). My emphasis will be on those components in the Steamworks documentation that directly relate to the facilitation and configuration of economic transactions, including who is entitled to which types of economic action on the platform. Firstly, I will address the key features of the Steamworks API in terms of market interactions. After this, I will describe in more detail the individual components of this framework for economic action. Finally, I will draw a general map of the way market interactions are shaped on the Steam platform and how different types of market actors – publishers, users, and Valve itself – are positioned within this framework.

Key features of the Steam business model

Two important features make the Steam platform business model stand out: the extension of economic action beyond the game store and the denunciation of advertising as a key source of revenue in favour of the microtransaction system. As concerns the extension of economic action beyond the game store, Steam's organization of market interactions on the platform differs considerably from its competitors. On Epic's game launcher, Steam's nearest competitor, economic transactions are limited to the game store and microtransactions within games. Players are invited to sell their own art assets, blueprints, code plugins, and so on in the Unreal marketplace, but no secondary market for items obtained in games exists at platform level. Many of the game titles put on sale obviously feature in-game economies and virtual currencies, but this economic action is kept within the boundaries of the individual game title: *Fortnite* skins stay within *Fortnite*. In comparison, by way of its 'inventory service', Steam enables the creation of a persistent inventory of game items linked to players' Steam accounts beyond the level of the individual game titles. This inventory is furthermore integrated with alternative markets on the platform, such as the Points Shop and the Steam community market. Publishers on the Steam platform can define specific game items as 'marketable' in the inventory service, and if they do so, players will be able to list these items on the community market directly from their Steam inventory. In this way, skins obtained from *Counter-Strike: Global Offensive* and *PlayerUnknown's Battlegrounds* can be accessed in the Steam inventory and listed on the Steam community market. Admittedly, Epic does allow players to earn money on item sales in the Unreal Engine Marketplace. Yet, as the name indicates, this is a market for freelance developers creating new assets using the Unreal game engine and selling them on the Unreal engine market, rather than a secondary market for players reselling items from their inventory. (For a more elaborate comparison of the two platforms, see Thorhauge and Nielsen, 2021.) Thus, the strategic expansion of market interactions beyond the game store represents one analytical lens through which the platform features can be analysed.

As concerns the denunciation of advertising, it is specifically pointed out in the Steamworks documentation that: 'Steam does not support paid ads or referral/affiliate revenue from showing ads to other games and/or products or services. If your game's revenue relies on advertising on other platforms, you will need to find a new model to ship on Steam'.[1] Of course, it is perfectly possible to put content into games that advertise a product or name a sponsor, but the Steam platform does not provide a system for showing or targeting ads in the same way that YouTube or the App Store have built this into their platforms and business models. Instead, the documentation proceeds, 'you could consider having your game be a single purchase or making it free-to-play with microtransactions and additional content as DLC', and particularly, microtransactions are pushed at several levels. The platform supports multiple ways of integrating microtransactions into the game experience through the game, the inventory service, the workshop, and from third-party web pages, and the documentation provides detailed implementation guides for doing this. The sheer number of possible paths into using the microtransaction system indicates that this is a major business emphasis, in addition to the classic retail market of the Steam store. Moreover, it is explicitly pointed out that the Steam platform does not put any limits on the ways in which microtransactions are integrated into the games and business models:

> Steam places no restrictions on what you sell or how you sell it, nor does it preclude the use of whatever other mechanisms your game has for selling items. Its purpose is to bring a common payment experience that user's (sic) are familiar with from the Steam platform into your game and allow them to easily spend their Steam wallet value on your products.[2]

In short: do whatever you want, just use microtransactions. Thus, the microtransaction system and its integration with the Steam Wallet can be considered the core features supporting the strategic expansion of market interactions on the platform. In the subsequent sections, I will describe some of the key components making up the Steam platform economy, as this can be deduced from the Steamworks documentation: the Steam store, the extended marketplaces, and the enabling of markets beyond the steam platform.

The Steam store and its preferred business models

To begin with the Steam store, this aspect of the platform takes a central position in terms of volume and visibility. Online retail has been a key business emphasis from the platform's early beginnings and remains a key source of revenue today. The store rests on a relatively traditional retail model, where a publisher offers a product to a customer at a fixed price. Players cannot resell games or game items in this market and if they wish to sell their own creations, they will have to 'turn themselves into publishers', joining the Steamworks distribution programme and paying the app deposit fee. A broad range of tools and advice are given to help game publishers find their customers and make a business, but as mentioned in the previous section, some business models are preferred over others. The Steam store does not provide a system for showing or targeting ads, while it welcomes paid for as well as free game titles and allows developers to switch between the two. Moreover, microtransactions are promoted while subscription-based models are possible but discouraged and not fully supported by the Steam store. The reason given is that players are generally less willing to accept such ongoing payments, which may very well be the case, but it may also be that the subscription model is not sufficient with regard to targeting and making a business out of diverse user segments (Hamari and Järvinen, 2011), that is, with regard to promoting microtransactions. A simple illustration of the Steam store as a component of the Steam platform economy is given (see Figure 6.1).

The publisher provides games and content and earns revenue by way of game sales or microtransactions when the consumer downloads games and content and pays by way of their Steam Wallet. Valve earns 30 per cent of the transactions taking place. This is more or less the business model that could be deduced from the press release when the platform was launched in 2003, and which was realized in the following years as Valve managed to attract a critical mass of publishers and players. The most important alteration is the introduction of microtransactions in 2012, which turned the individual game into an additional retail window, and which is also a growing business model on competing platforms such as PlayStation. In comparison to other entertainment platforms such as Facebook and YouTube, the most striking

Figure 6.1: The Steam store

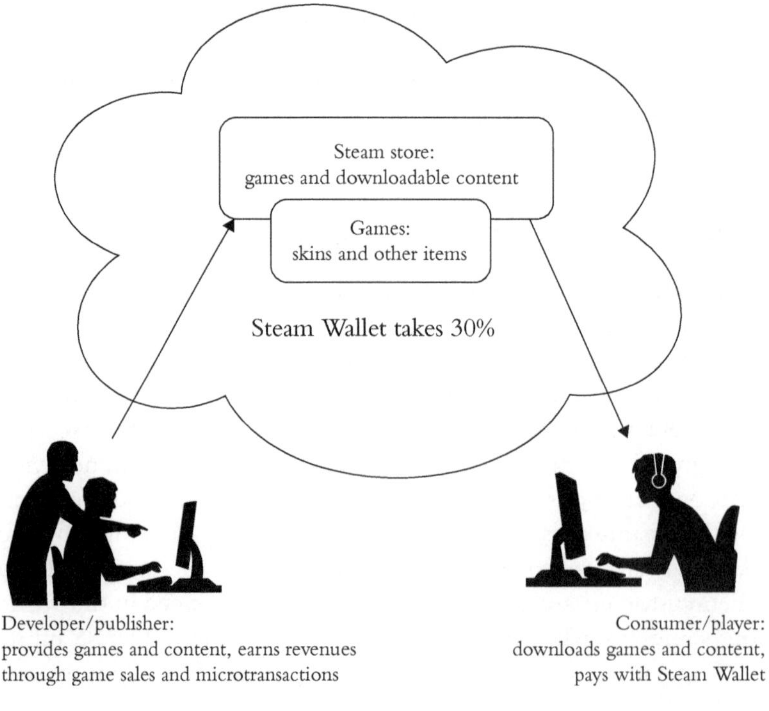

Steam store:
games and downloadable content

Games:
skins and other items

Steam Wallet takes 30%

Developer/publisher:
provides games and content, earns revenues
through game sales and microtransactions

Consumer/player:
downloads games and content,
pays with Steam Wallet

feature is the absence of advertising as a revenue model. Valve has deliberately rejected this business model from the Steam platform in favour of alternative business emphases revolving around the expansion of economic transactions.

Marketplaces on Steam

The 'derivate' markets of the Steam community workshop and community market can be interpreted as a strategic attempt at expanding the amount of economic transactions of which Steam can earn a share. If a game publisher decides to open a workshop in relation to a specific game title and to enable item sales, and players choose to make use of this option, Valve will once again earn a share of sales by way of the Steam Wallet. The incentive for the game publisher may just be to embrace and consolidate the games' fan community, but it may also be a strategic approach to getting new content into the game. In this way, the workshop can support the generation of both value in the form of content that can be monetized elsewhere and value in the form of direct economic transactions (see Chapter 5 and Figure 6.2). The Steam workshop receives a fair amount of emphasis in the Steam platform documentation. It was introduced in 2011 as an addition to *Team Fortress 2* and functions as a hub where players can share their own creations and browse through/subscribe to others. This activity of adding content, or modding, has a long history in online gaming at a general level and in the history of Valve/Steam more specifically. Indeed, the original *Counter-Strike*, which was later followed by *Counter-Strike: Global Offensive*, Valve's most successful game title to date (and the most played game on the platform), was born out of such efforts. In this way, it is no surprise that modding receives special attention on the platform. What is interesting, though, is the specific ways in which this activity is transformed into value by way of the platform features. In the platform documentation, a distinction is made between 'ready-to-use workshops' and 'curated workshops', the latter implying that the game publisher actively 'curates' contributions made by players and integrates them into their games. In this way, the Steam workshop promotes a direct integration of player-created content into those game titles that are sold in the game store or monetized through microtransactions. Moreover, a rather controversial design choice on the platform was the introduction of 'paid mods' in 2015. As I describe in Chapter 5, this spawned a great deal of controversy at the time as it challenged the idea of modding as a non-market mode of game development and effectively commodified what was considered goods created and thus owned by the community (Joseph, 2018). Nevertheless, the option of paid mods in the Steam community workshop is still available and is actively used by approximately 90 game titles on the platform at the time of writing (see Chapter 7).

As a context of economic exchange, the Steam community workshop is rather ambiguous. The majority of game titles with a workshop have chosen the 'ready-to-use' form where neither item curation nor item sales are employed as a means to transform active player contributions into value for the developer (and Valve). In these cases, the workshop stays in accordance with the traditional notion of modding as a hobby and a community phenomenon that should not be mixed up with market interactions. In the minority of cases where emphasis is placed on curation, player contributions are made subject to quality measures on behalf of the developer, turning the modder into a compensated or non-compensated 'employee'. Finally, the choice to integrate the item sale feature introduces market interactions directly into the modding activity, as described in Chapter 5. In practice, this involves an integration with the Steam inventory service and microtransactions API, once again leading economic activities through the Steam Wallet, as illustrated in Figure 6.2.

While the Steam community workshop gets a lengthy introduction followed by a detailed implementation guide, there is close to no description of the community market. It is mentioned briefly in the introduction to Steam trading cards and inventory service, but new developers will have to search the documentation relatively thoroughly to figure out how exactly to make their items available in the community market. At the same time, however, there is considerable emphasis on the Steam community market

Figure 6.2: The Steam community workshop

Specific game title

Steam community workshop for specific game title

Steam Wallet takes 30%

Developer/publisher:
curates content, earns a share

Consumer/player:
provides or downloads content,
pays with Steam Wallet

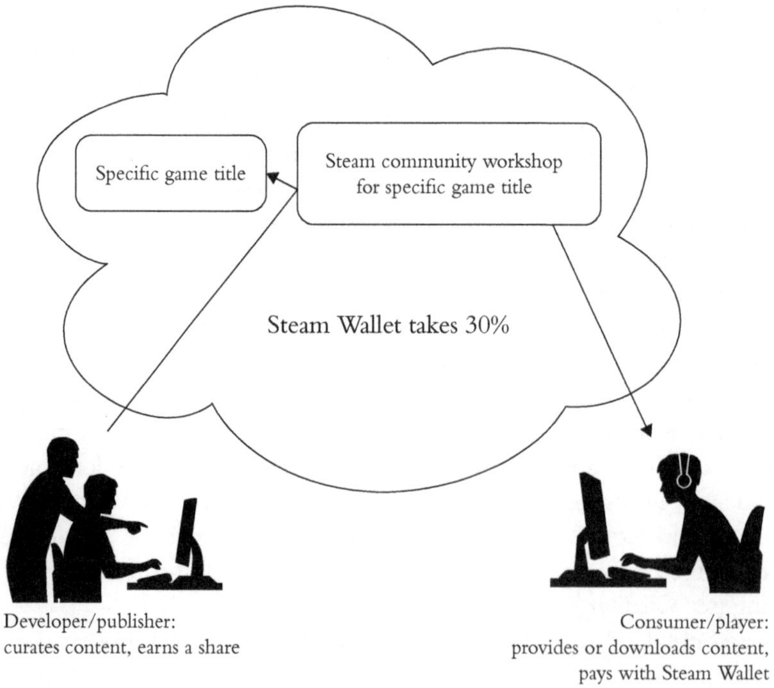

in the API reference, where a broad range of data and actions related to the community market is made available. In the Steam client, the community market is presented under community features at the same level as the community workshop. This is rather contradictory, but as I will return to in a moment, this may be an indication of the Steam community market's role in Valve's general business strategy.

In the Steam community market, consumers/players are not given the option of adding content to the market. Instead, they can trade items that game publishers have decided to make marketable (see Figure 6.3). The Steam inventory service API allows third-party developers to integrate the platform's inventory functionalities so that items from the game will appear in the inventory linked to players' Steam accounts. Relatively deep into this API reference appears the option of marking items as either *tradable* –players can trade the item with other players via their inventory – or *marketable* – players can list the items in the community market and earn Steam credits that are stored in their Steam Wallet. Two important features of this market context should be highlighted here. Firstly, this is a market for a very specific type of product, marketable items, and players will not be able to list anything else, such as games they don't play any longer or items they have created themselves. It is ultimately the game developers that decide what should be traded in this market, while players are only given the option of buying or selling them as part of their attempt to obtain desired items, build a collection, or perhaps turn trading into a metagame in its own right. Secondly, and very importantly, prices are presented in conventional currencies. While players will not be able to withdraw these dollars or euros from their Steam Wallet, only to spend it on the platform, it still adds tremendously to the convertibility of the traded items as it makes their value translatable into external value systems. In combination, these two features have turned the Steam community market into a sort of 'investment game' forming the basis for some of the 'extra-platform' activities that will be addressed in Chapter 8. An illustration is given here (see Figure 6.3).

The absence of information on the Steam community market may be due to the relative simplicity regarding its technical implementation: developers will only have to tick the 'marketable box' in the inventory service, and then players will be able to trade the item in the community market (which, of course, is no guarantee that players will trade it). However, the absence of information on the community market may also be due to Valve not having an interest in getting too much competition in this specific market context. The dominance of Valve-owned games in the Steam community market is overwhelming – more than 65 per cent of unique items traded originate from these games at the time of writing – and it is likely that Valve prefer it this way because the trade that takes place in the community market is a primary source of revenue for these games (see next chapter). For instance,

Figure 6.3: The Steam community market

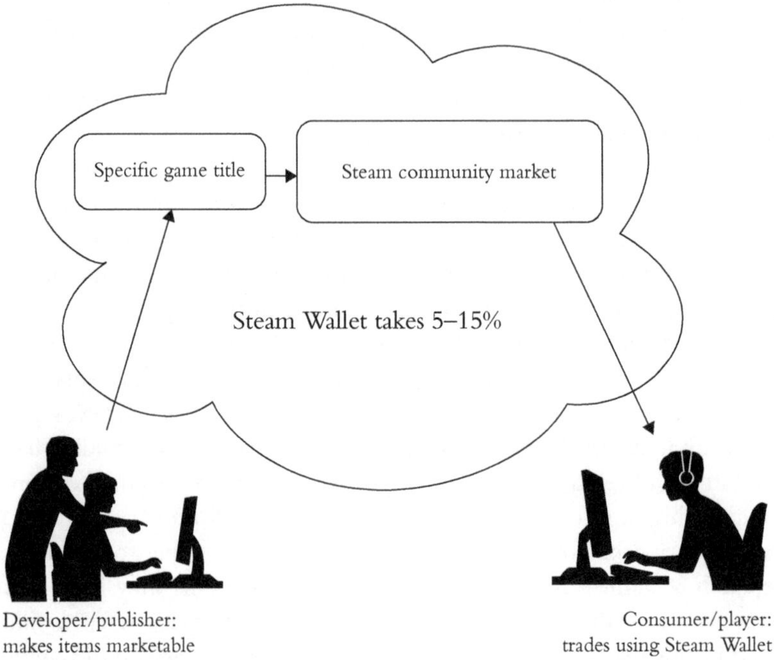

Developer/publisher:
makes items marketable

Consumer/player:
trades using Steam Wallet

Counter-Strike: Global Offensive is free in the Steam store and most items are earned through 'random drops' in the form of loot boxes. Players will only be able to open these boxes if they purchase a 'key' which will generate some income. Yet, as compared to the pricing of skins in competing game titles such as *Fortnite, Counter-Strike: Global Offensive* keys are relatively low priced, and it is likely that the primary business emphasis lies in the player trading in the Steam market, of which Valve/Steam earns a share (see Thorhauge and Nielsen, 2021, and Chapter 4, for a comparison of these business models). Moreover, the Steam community workshop is organized around the individual game titles and their dedicated fan communities, whereas the community market gathers items from all game titles that have made items marketable on Steam. While it is less likely that a dedicated *Skyrim* fan will switch to the *Counter-Strike: Global Offensive* workshop because it has more attractive items on sale, it is more likely that items from *Counter-Strike: Global Offensive* in the Steam community market will have to compete with items from non–Valve game titles in the 'metagame of trading'.

All roads lead through the Steam Wallet

In the previous sections, I have described the components of the Steam platform economy: the store as well as alternative contexts of economic exchange. At the same time, I have addressed how some of these components are explained at length in the Steamworks documentation, while others are systematically absent. While the store takes a central position in terms of visibility and volume, and while extended implementation guides are provided for the microtransaction system and the Steam workshop, it is difficult to find any descriptions of the way the Steam community market can be implemented into the games that are sold on the platform. As I will return to in Chapter 8, this may be due to the way Valve handles competition between its own and competing game titles on the platform. Another component which is similarly absent from the Steamworks documentation is the Steam Wallet, to which players can upload funds through various types of payment systems. The Steam Wallet was introduced in 2010, along with micropayments, and represents the key entry into this system. If game publishers want to implement the microtransaction system, they will have to use the Steam Wallet, and if players wish to buy an item in a game, they must have funds in their Wallet. Similarly, all transactions on the Steam community markets take place through the Steam Wallet. As concerns the store, it is possible to buy games using various credit cards, but the Steam Wallet appears as the default option. In this way, the Wallet can be defined as that key feature of all contexts of economic exchange available on the platform, as illustrated in Figure 6.4.

As the map illustrates, the Steam Wallet represents the basic payment system no matter the character of economic transaction taking place. Moreover, the map identifies the types of economic transaction taking place in accordance with the way game publishers as well as gamers are positioned as market actors. Publishers provide games and other contents to the game store and earn sales from this. They may also make items marketable in the Steam community market, but they do not act as sellers in this context. Yet, it is only game items they have made marketable by the publisher that can be traded here. Finally, publishers may choose to use the Steam community workshop to get new content into their games, either through a process of curation or by way of 'ready-to-use items', and they may turn the option of 'paid mods' into an additional source of revenue. As concerns players, they can buy games and other content in the store, but they are not allowed to take the role of seller in this context. In the community market, on the other hand, players can take the role of buyers as well as sellers, though trading is limited to items made marketable by game publishers. In the context of the Steam community workshop, players will be able to download/upload items and buy/earn sales from items depending on the way the publisher has decided to set up the workshop. In any case, the 'workshop-as-store' will be handled by the game publisher, and revenues from sales will be shared between players, publishers, and Valve. In this way, the Steam platform effectively defines what Fligstein

Figure 6.4: Steam's tangled markets

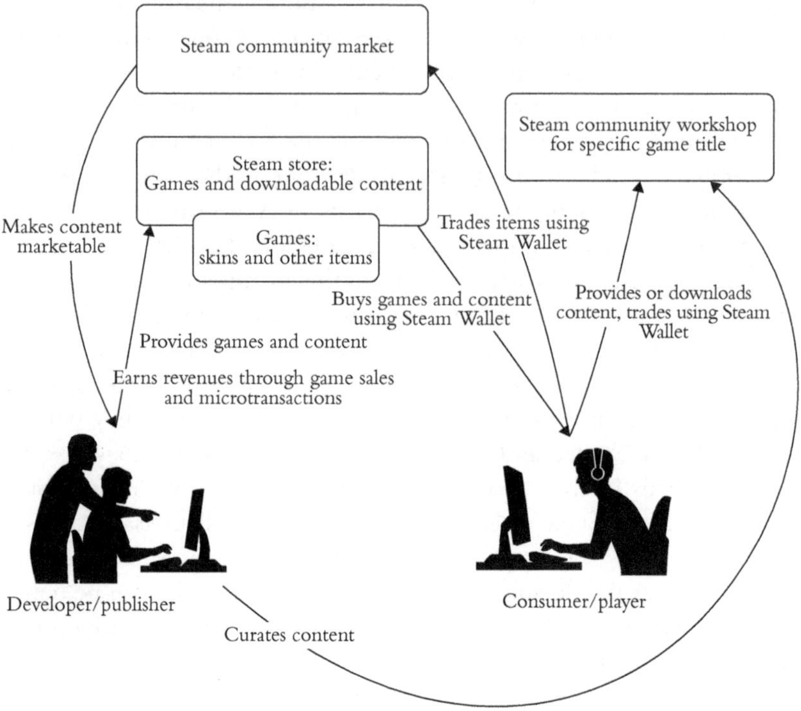

All roads lead through the Steam Wallet

(1996, 2001) refers to as rules of transaction, that is, who is able to trade what under which circumstances?

As concerns this last point, another fact systematically unavailable in the Steamworks documentation is Valve's relative share of the economic transactions taking place. Not in the introduction to the store, the microtransaction system, the option of paid mods in the workshop, or anywhere else in the Steamworks documentation is mentioned the platform owner's relative share of sales, or how sales are divided between game publishers, players, and Valve. To obtain this information, it is necessary to look for it elsewhere. Steam's relative share of sales in the Steam store became a topic in game journalism when Epic Games decided to launch a competing platform in the form of the Epic Games Store, with a lower share of transactions as a competitive parameter. While Valve earns a 30 per cent share of sales in the Steam store, Epic earns 12 per cent.[3] Possibly due to this challenge, Valve later agreed to lower its share when revenue gets over a certain level so that the split goes down to 25 per cent for sales beyond $10 million and 20 per cent for sales beyond $50 million.[4] As I will get back to in the next chapter, this obviously benefits large publishers and can be interpreted as an attempt to keep 'incumbent publishers' on the platform to retain a critical mass.

While these numbers primarily refer to the share of game sales and microtransactions, Valve's share of economic transactions in the Steam community market and community workshop takes a bit more detective work. As concerns the community market, Valve takes a general transaction fee of 5 per cent paid by the buyer and another 10 per cent game-specific fee in the case of certain game titles (which are all, notably, published by Valve itself), according to the Steam community market FAQ.[5] According to Joseph (2018), Valve would earn 30 per cent of revenues from the sale of paid mods in the original *The Elder Scrolls V: Skyrim* setup, but it is hard to find any official account of this or of what Valve gets today. Nonetheless, 'all roads lead through the Steam Wallet'. Every transaction, no matter if it is initiated in the store, the market, or the workshop, will pass through the Steam Wallet and Valve will earn a share, however small. This is very likely the rationale behind the strategic expansion of economic transactions on the Steam platform and an indication of Valve's specific approach to 'monetizing the long tail' (O'Reilly, 2007) of social connectivity.

In Chapter 3, I suggested the concept of tangled markets to address the specific ways in which contemporary digital platforms enable and shape market interactions. In tangled markets, I refer to complex market contexts containing several interconnected and mutually dependent markets and domains of interaction. The tangled market of the Steam platform includes the original storefront as well as the community market and the community workshop, which may, insofar as economic actors choose to make use of them, contribute to the overall platform economy in a range of ways, for instance, by adding content to the games or raising the number of microtransactions. However, the relative amount and value of these transactions depend considerably on the way actors choose to operate on the platform, such as publishers' pricing strategies in the game store and choices to include the Steam community market and community workshop in their business emphasis, and players' willingness to accept these strategies and play their part. In Chapter 7, I will combine an analysis of available API data and additional data collected from the platform interface to analyse how game titles and game publishers are distributed across these contexts and their impact on the platform as measured by player counts.

7

Economic Actors on the Steam Platform

In Chapter 4, I define markets as fields of strategic action based on Fligstein's theoretical framework (2001). I point out that Fligstein offers a relevant approach to analysing the interplay between diverse actors in a market context. While Granovetter points out that economic actors are also social actors enmeshed in social networks (1985), Fligstein describes the 'politics' that are played out within and between firms on markets as fields of strategic action. These politics concern 'intra-firm' negotiations to settle on specific 'conceptions of control' that set the direction for said firms' strategies in the market (2001: 35). They also concern the specific 'market orders' that emerge between companies in market contexts as a way of handling competition between them (2001: 16). Thus, Fligstein, along with Beckert, points out that competition does not represent an ideal state of affairs but rather a problem to be handled through various kinds of coordination. Indeed, the state of competition often heralded as the ideal in classic economics is a characteristic of emerging markets and is typically replaced with more stable orders where 'incumbents' divide the world between them to keep 'challengers' out as a market matures. In this chapter, I will analyse the way game titles and publishers are distributed across the different contexts of economic exchange offered on the Steam platform from this perspective. Firstly, I will discuss the different types of market actors present on the Steam platform and how Valve's combined status as a game developer, game publisher, and platform owner calls for a reinterpretation of Fligstein's framework. As an extension of this, I will map in more detail how these challengers and incumbents transform the platform as an 'environment of expected use' (Light et al, 2018) into a specific market order. I discuss how this market order can be interpreted as a way of handling competition and how the Steam platform design can be said to 'materialize' a specific governance structure. Before I embark on this analysis, however, I will present the data that forms the basis of this analysis.

A few words on method

To analyse the market order on the Steam platform, I have collected data using the Steam API and augmented this with data collected directly from the user interface. As I pointed out in Chapter 6, the Steam platform offers a voluminous API in Steamworks, and this allows for a collection of data on all public app IDs.[1] The API gives access to a range of data in relation to individual game titles, such as publisher, price, release date, availability of DLC, and use of in-app purchases.[2] It does not include data on game titles' presence in alternative contexts of economic exchange such as the Steam workshop and community market, though, so I have collected these data directly from the individual games' workshop pages and the Steam community market interface. From the workshop pages, I have collected data on features that have been enabled in relation to specific game titles and the number of uploaded items. From the market interface, I have collected data on the number of unique items made marketable in the Steam community market. Of course, game publishers may have made more items available than those that can be detected from the market interface, since items will only show up in cases where players have actually chosen to make use of these features. Nevertheless, the relative differences in the number of unique marketable items can give some indication of different game titles' emphasis in this context of economic exchange.

The list of public app IDs collected from the API amounts to more than 160,000. Obviously, not all of these apps are regular games, so a first step in the analysis has been to decide what to include. I have settled on apps of the type 'game' and 'mod', while I have excluded additional content such as videos and soundtracks. Moreover, I have limited the dataset to those games and mods that have a proper release date to filter out unfinished and abandoned projects. These choices have left me with a dataset of approximately 58,000 game titles covering all games and mods that have been published on the platform from its introduction in 2003 to the end of 2022. Not all these games are being played, so I have collected additional data on player numbers in April 2023.[3] as an indication of these titles' relative impact on the platform using the player count API.[4] These data show that about 13,000 of the game titles are being played by at least one player during the time of data collection and that a small number of game titles, primarily published by Valve, draw the bulk of players on the platform. They also show that 1694 game titles have an associated workshop page in the Steam community workshop and only 221 game titles have made items marketable in the community market at the time of data collection.

My analysis concerns the relative business emphasis of individual game titles across the game store, workshop, and market, and thus the main purpose of initial data processing and visualization has been to categorize available data in ways that give an indication of such emphases. Regarding store data, I have categorized the game titles in accordance with their emphasis on initial point of sale (whether they are free or not) and upselling (whether additional content can be purchased from the store or through in-app purchases). This gives me four groups featuring either initial point of sale only, upselling only, a combination of these, or none of these. Regarding workshop data, I have categorized game titles with a workshop page in accordance with the features that have been enabled. Most game titles with a workshop page have only enabled 'ready-to-use items', indicating a non-intensive use of the workshop business-wise, while a smaller group have included features for curating items and/or selling them in the workshop, demonstrating a more intensive use in terms of integrating player contributions into the general value chain of the game title. Hence, I have categorized game titles in accordance with this. Regarding market data, I have identified the threshold number of items between 'the long tail and the tiny head' to be approximately 800 unique marketable items and used this as an indication of game titles' relative emphasis in this context of economic exchange (see Figure 7.1).

I have developed my own scripts for collecting and analysing data in RStudio and these as well as accompanying documentation can be accessed on the book's resource page.

Market power or marketplace power? Economic actors in the game market

In Chapter 4, I introduce Fligstein's notion of markets as strategic fields of action populated by incumbents and challengers. According to Fligstein, a certain market order will emerge as a market matures which can ultimately be defined as a hierarchy of market actors. Typically, a few 'incumbent' firms will dominate the market and orient themselves towards each other rather than towards the challengers operating in the market as well. Strategic action in this market order is directed towards the continued existence of the firm by avoiding the detrimental effects of competition. That is, instead of classic economy's 'rational man', Fligstein's market actor is a 'safeguarding man' acting strategically to ensure a stable social world for the sake of the continued existence of the firm (Sparsam, 2016). This strategic action is guided by incumbent firms' conception of control, a relatively ambiguous term which is in some cases used for historical periodization (Fligstein, 1990) and in others defined in a micro-sociological manner as 'local knowledge' and 'toolbox tactics' (Fligstein, 2001: 35). In the context of the game market, conception of control can be used to define historical trends such as the market dominance of game console owners in the 1980s and the 1990s and the shift toward freemium and mobile gaming from the 2010s onwards, which indicates how changing market actors employ highly distinctive

Figure 7.1: Items in the Steam community market

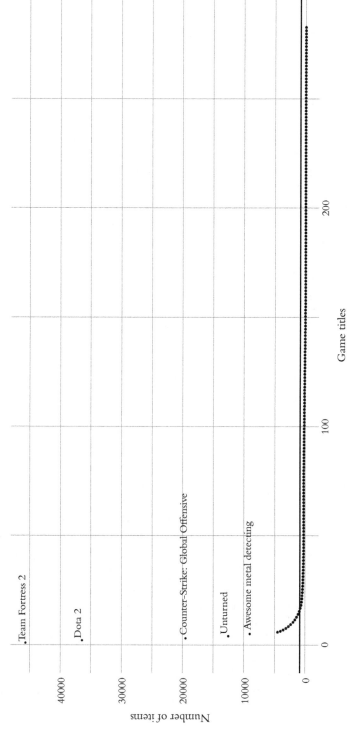

Note: Black line refers to threshold value of 800 unique marketable items.

ways of transforming technological affordances and gaming practices into businesses (see Chapter 2). Conception of control can also be operationalized as the strategic action performed by market actors on a day-to-day basis, such as the way different complementors and micro-entrepreneurs (Van Dijck et al, 2018) on the Steam platform transform platform features into specific business emphases. In my analysis, I will demonstrate how the relative emphasis on store, workshop, and market depends on the type of publisher in question, that is, Valve itself, large publishers, independent developers, or amateurs. As an extension of this, I will discuss how this defines their position in the Steam platform market order and beyond.

Defining who are incumbents and who are challengers in this context is a difficult endeavour and depends on the analytical focus. Valve is an incumbent in the market of PC gaming, where the Steam platform dominates. Yet, in the wider game market, PC gaming only accounts for approximately 20 per cent of revenue, while console and mobile gaming account for 40 per cent each.[5] Those who control the dominating gaming consoles (Sony, Microsoft, and Nintendo) and the markets for mobile gaming (Apple, Google, and Tencent) hold considerably more power in these contexts. Indeed, in the contemporary global game market, incumbents have adeptly shared the PC and mobile markets between them, yet still compete at a number of levels. For instance, some companies participate as publishers in each other's markets, such as Google and Microsoft publishing game titles on the Steam platform, while others don't for reasons of competition, such as Epic. Indeed, it is important to define whether competition is between platforms and their storefronts (Steam game store, Epic game store, Xbox game store, and so on) or between specific game titles with the same type of gameplay (*Fortnite* versus *Apex Legends, Dota 2* versus *League of Legends*).

Valve is simultaneously a platform owner competing with other storefronts in the PC gaming market, such as the Epic game store, and a game publisher competing with other game publishers in specific game segments, such as first-person shooters and MOBA game titles. In this way, it simultaneously has an interest in drawing key publishers to the Steam store to retain critical mass vis-à-vis competing storefronts, while avoiding direct competition between their own game titles and competing ones on the Steam platform. The other way around, other combined platform owners and game publishers may choose to be strategically non-present on the Steam platform in order not to 'cannibalize' their own storefronts. For instance, as I touch briefly upon in Chapter 4, EA, publisher of some of the most played and profitable game titles to date, opened the Origin store in 2011 as a competing storefront to the Steam game store. As part of this venture, EA withdrew most of its content from the Steam store so that players that played game titles from both publishers would have to have an account on both platforms. Yet, Origin did not manage to compete with Steam to the degree expected. In 2019,

EA and Steam resumed cooperation and key EA titles went back on Steam. At the time of writing, the Epic game store is the primary competitor to the Steam game store in the market of PC gaming, and for the same reason, Epic-published game titles are, with notable exceptions, not available on the Steam platform along with titles from other publishers that have chosen to take part in Epic's 'platform-exclusive' strategy. In this way, competition simultaneously takes place at the level of the storefront and the individual game titles, and the platform owners can be likened to sovereigns that strategically support and defend their home markets by being strategically present or non-present in certain contexts.

Economic actors in the Steam market order

Van Dijck et al point out that platforms are dependent on complementors, that is, 'organizations or individuals that provide products or services to end users through platforms' (2018: 17). These complementors can be organizations, public institutions, or firms, but they may also be 'micro-entrepreneurs', such as individuals renting out their car or apartment through the platform. Thus, the notion of complementors is a very broad term that does not allow for a further analysis of individual complementors' positions vis-à-vis other complementors and the platform itself. Instead, I will add the notions of 'meso-' and 'macro-entrepreneurs' to that of the 'micro-entrepreneur' to address the different types of positions actors may have in the Steam market order. Valve's combined position as platform owner and game publisher turns the company into more than an incumbent in the context of Steam. Indeed, Valve has the role of a state, defining institutional frameworks and rules of economic interaction through the platform features in the same manner as done by states and governments in much current writing on 'the architecture of markets' (Fligstein, 2001; Vogel, 2018). The continuous evolution of the Steam platform can be interpreted from this perspective as a strategic tweaking of its features to shape market interactions in the same way as states and governments continuously update legal frameworks and regulate the monetary system to ensure a desirable state in the market. The other way around, all the other actors populating the Steam market order cannot be reduced to a single category of 'challengers' or 'complementors'. As I point out in the previous section, the strategic presence and non-presence of EA and Epic respectively are key to the Steam platform market due to their role and relative power in the wider game market. Thus, it makes more sense to refer to these as well as other incumbents in the wider game market as 'macro-entrepreneurs' that Valve has a certain interest in attracting to the platform along with their flagship game titles and gaming communities, while the meso- and micro-entrepreneurs of 'indie' developers and amateurs represent another kind of economic interest as a 'customer segment' in the

Steam store. Accordingly, when analysing the distribution of game titles and their publishers across the Steam platform, as well as their relative emphasis in the different contexts of economic exchange, it is necessary to distinguish between different types of actors. In the subsequent section, I will demonstrate how the business emphasis of Valve as the 'platform ruler' differs from that of the game companies in the global top 25[6] as well as the broader group of meso- and micro-entrepreneurs operating on the platform. As an extension of this, I will discuss how this can be interpreted as a way of handling 'the competition problem', and how the platform features materially govern and shape the Steam market order.

The business emphases of market actors on Steam

The most striking characteristic of the collected data is the relative dominance of Valve-published game titles in the context of the Steam community workshop and community market. While the micro- and meso-entrepreneurs on the Steam platform tend to place their primary emphasis on initial point of sale in the game store, and the macro-entrepreneurs (in this context defined as companies in the global top 25) to a higher degree combine this with upselling, Valve-published games focus more on upselling, that is, they can be downloaded for free in the Steam store, and strongly dominate the Steam community workshop and community market in terms of the number of available items in these contexts.

To begin with the game titles' emphasis in the Steam store, Figure 7.2 shows the relative emphasis of Valve-published games titles vis-à-vis publishers in the global top 25 and other publishers in terms of their emphasis on initial point of sale only, initial point of sale and upselling, upselling only, and none of these. The latter covers a diverse group of game titles, including mods, titles that are still under development (*VRChat*, *tModLoader*), and games that have been withdrawn from the Steam store (*Rocket League*). As can be seen from the diagram, Valve-published game titles to a larger degree put their emphasis on upselling, while top 25 publishers combine initial point of sale and upselling.

This is not very surprising since upselling is an obvious way of monetizing the large following that characterizes these publishers' game titles. Yet, Valve-published titles to a much larger degree use the Steam community workshop and community market as part of their upselling strategy. As can be seen from Figure 7.3, other large publishers are close to non-present in the contexts of the Steam community workshop and community market. Measured in terms of enabled features in the Steam community workshop, Valve-published games use this relatively more intensely, and measured in terms of number of published items, Valve-published games dominate both contexts immensely. Indeed, while seven out of 1694 game titles with a

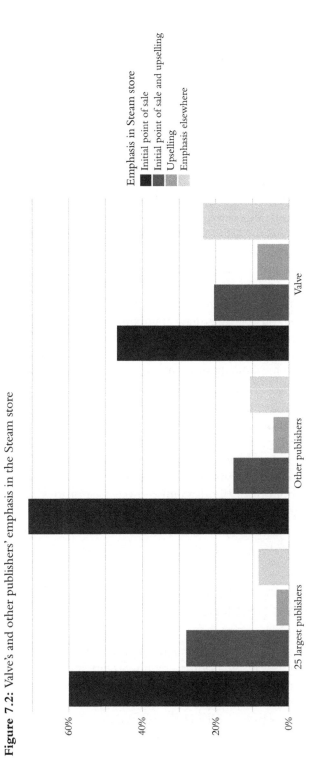

Figure 7.2: Valve's and other publishers' emphasis in the Steam store

workshop page are published by Valve, 3,208,765 out of 13,087,061, or 25 per cent, of the total number of items uploaded to the workshop are uploaded to Valve-published titles. Similarly, while three out of 221 game titles in the Steam community market are published by Valve, 101,852 out of 157,881, or 65 per cent, in the Steam community market are associated with Valve-published titles.

In short, while Steam offers a 'palette of monetization options' for publishers selling their games on the platform, publishers are distributed unevenly across these. Micro- and meso-entrepreneurs primarily use the platform for initial point of sale in the game store, while large publishers combine this with upselling. To both types of actors, the Steam platform primarily seems to be a storefront. On the other hand, Valve to a lesser degree base their revenue models on initial point of sale and to a larger degree on upselling grounded in player-driven economies, as these are enabled in the Steam community workshop and community market.

As I wrote in the introduction to this chapter, approximately 13,000 game titles are being played by at least one player at the time of writing. Moreover, the top 100 titles draw approximately three quarters of the total player count, with Valve-published games taking the lead. Figure 7.4 shows this data along with year of release and emphasis in the Steam game store. As can be seen from the diagram, three game titles published by Valve draw the bulk of player counts: *Counter-Strike: Global Offensive*, *Dota 2*, and *Team Fortress 2* along with *PlayerUnknown Battleground* and *Rust*. These titles also display a strong emphasis on upselling through the Steam community workshop and community market. *PlayerUnknown's Battlegrounds* has a relatively high degree of presence in the Steam community market while *Rust* combines initial point of sale and upselling. The large group of game titles at the bottom of the diagram shows a 'sea of grey', indicating that micro-entrepreneurs, that is, indie developers and amateurs drawing small player counts, primarily base their revenue models on initial point of sale in the Steam store.

The steam market order as a solution to the competition problem

As the diagrams in the previous section indicate, publishers are distributed unevenly across the different contexts of economic exchange on the Steam platform. In this way, the platform represents different types of markets and business contexts to different types of actors. To the micro-, meso-, and macro-entrepreneurs operating on the platform, Steam is basically a storefront running in accordance with a classic retail model and a window to engage with the gaming audience. The primary difference as compared to competing storefronts is the denunciation of advertising as a revenue model, which

Figure 7.3: Valve's and other publishers' emphasis in the Steam community workshop and community market

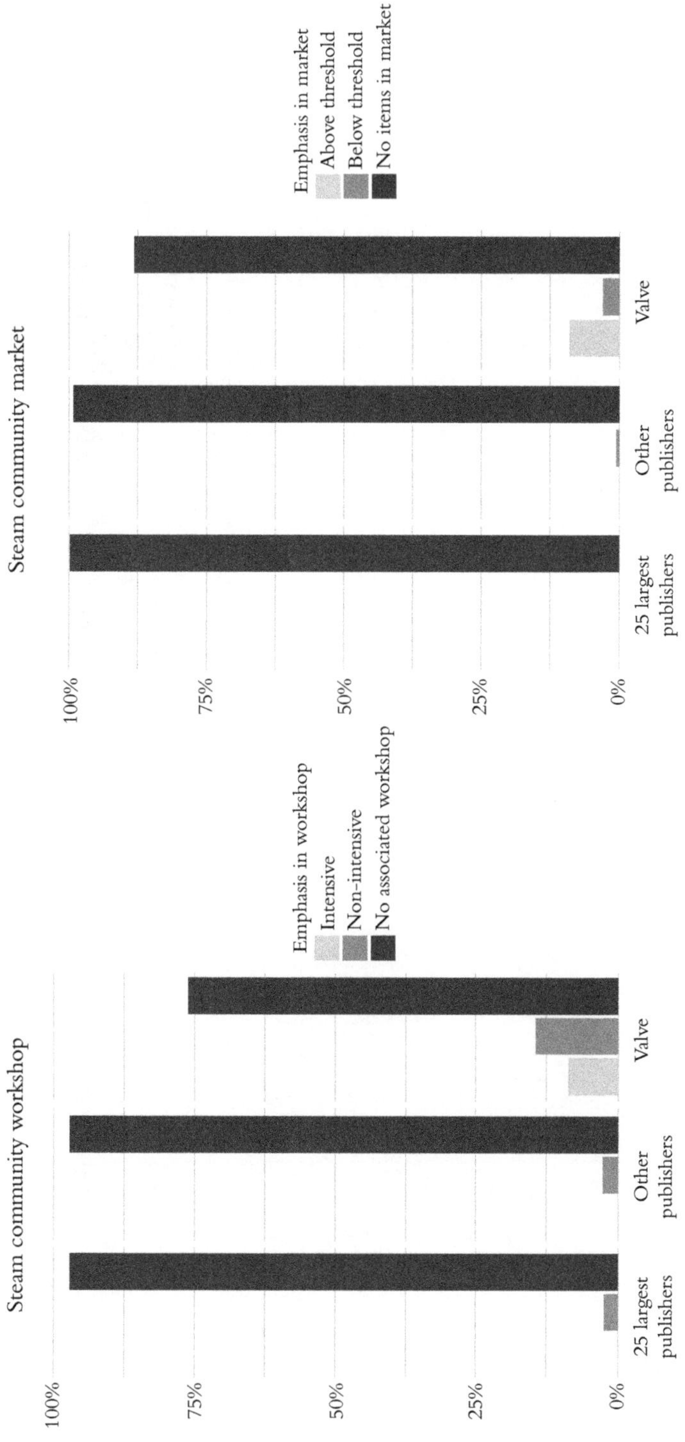

Steam community workshop

Steam community market

Emphasis in workshop
- Intensive
- Non-intensive
- No associated workshop

Emphasis in market
- Above threshold
- Below threshold
- No items in market

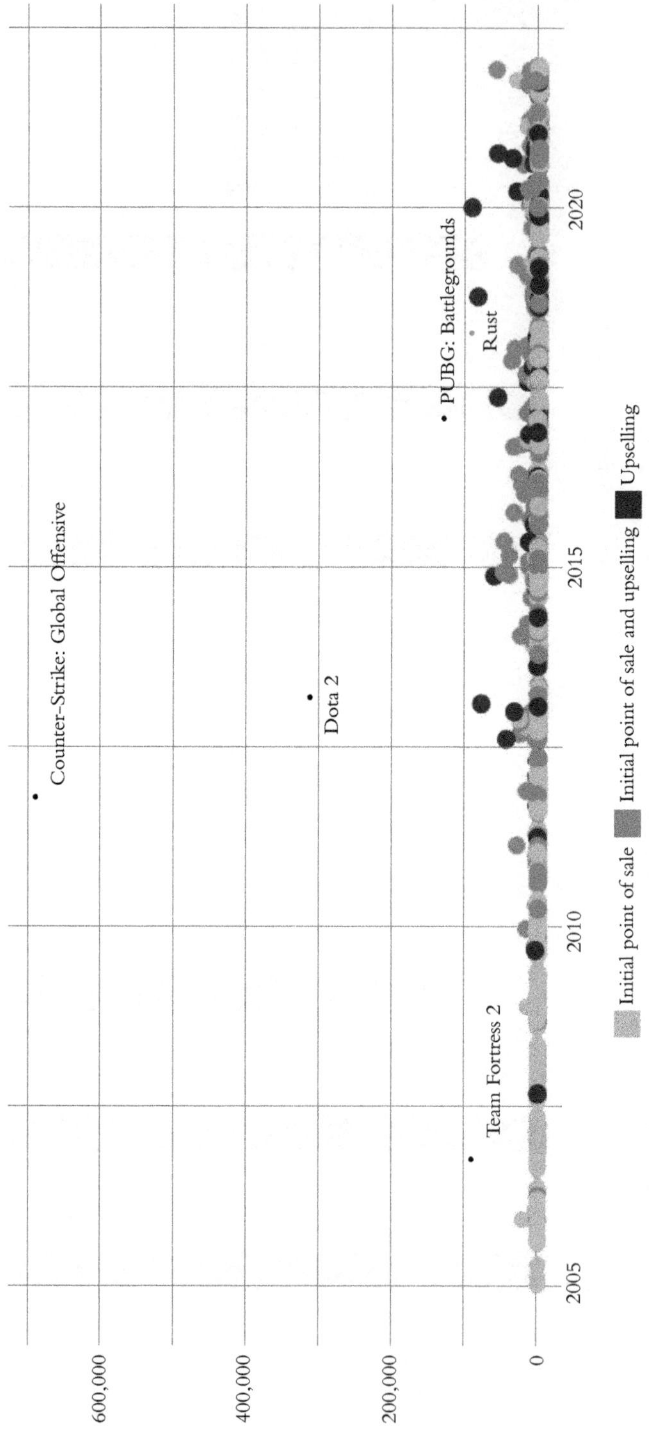

Figure 7.4: Game titles on Steam as measured by player number, year of release, and emphasis on the Steam store

represents a key business stategy in the storefronts of dominating platform actors (see Chapter 2). To Valve itself, the Steam platform is an assembly of different contexts of economic exchange allowing for the monetization of playbour and player-driven economies (see Chapter 4). While a few Valve-published game titles do compete with other publishers' titles in accordance with the principles of classic retail, Valves flagship titles – *Team Fortress 2*, *Counter-Strike: Global Offensive*, and *Dota 2* – place their business emphasis on monetization of playbour and player-driven economies in other contexts on the platform.

There are several possible explanations of this pattern: history, critical mass, platform advantages, and the competition problem. As concerns the first, the Steam community workshop and community market were both introduced in relation to specific Valve-published game titles and made accessible for other publishers at a later point in time (see Chapter 6). This head start may explain part of their current dominance in these contexts. As concerns the second, monetizing playbour and player-driven economies in these contexts may depend on the attainment of critical mass. Increasing revenue-paid mods or player trading is only possible once a certain following has been established. If there are too few players to establish a dynamic modding community or community of traders, opening a workshop page or handling marketable items may just not be worth the effort. In this way, the relatively higher presence of *PlayerUnknown's Battlegrounds* and Valve itself may just be due to the relatively higher player counts turning this into a viable option. Yet, another explanation has to do with Valve's platform advantages. It basically earns more on each transaction taking place in the Steam community workshop and community market as compared to other publishers in these contexts. Since sales are split between players, publishers, and platform, and since Valve in the case of its own titles takes the role of both, the economic incentive for using these contexts is obviously higher. Finally, Valve-published game titles' relative emphasis in the alternative contexts of economic exchange can be interpreted as a way of handling the competition problem.

In Chapter 3, I introduced Fligstein's notion of markets as a field of strategic action and Becker's idea of coordination problems in markets. One of Fligstein's main points is that competition does not represent an ideal state of affairs but rather a problem that has to be handled, and in a similar manner, Beckert points to competition as one key coordination problem (2009). Valve's introduction of alternative contexts of economic exchange and a relatively higher emphasis in these contexts can be interpreted as a way of handling competition through 'diversification', reshaping its business focus to avoid direct competition with other key actors on the platform. As I point out at the beginning of this chapter, Steam has an interest in attracting and maintaining large publishers in the wider game market to its platform to ensure that its game store can compete with other storefronts in the field. At the same time, Valve as a publisher finds itself in direct competition with these publishers, and one obvious way of handling this problem is to change the business in ways that reduce the amount of direct competition. By making its games 'free-to-play', Valve opts out of the competition for users' funds in the Steam store and places its business elsewhere. In this way, the company can simultaneously run its storefront and publish its games on the platform without conflicting interests.

The Steam platform as market governance

Another important aspect of the analysis presented in the previous sections is how the market order is shaped by the platform design. As I point out in Chapter 3, market scholars, with a few notable exceptions, tend to ignore the material conditions of markets as an important aspect of how they work. Donald MacKenzie addresses the 'material political economy of algorithmic trading' (2018), and Marie-France Garcia-Parpet mentions how the physical architecture of the market she studies expresses a certain ideal of what represents a perfect market (2007). Apart from these exceptions, 'the architecture of markets' (Fligstein, 2001) is seldom taken literally by market scholars, and 'marketcraft' (Vogel, 2018) typically concerns organizational and regulatory aspects of markets rather than their material foundations. Yet, as Srnicek points out, one key aspect of platforms is the way they shape market interactions through their architecture (2017), and the analysis presented in this and Chapter 6 can be seen as an example of what this means in practice. In Chapter 6, I identify the different contexts of economic exchange as can be deduced from the Steamworks documentation, and how they define specific rules of transactions, such as who can trade what with whom and under which conditions. As an extension of this, I map the diverse contexts of economic exchange that make up the Steam platform economy.

In this chapter, I have analysed how different actors in the PC game market populate this map, and as the analysis indicates, different actors indeed seem to utilize this space in very different manners. The monetization of player-driven economies is primarily practised by the platform owner, while the 'macro-entrepreneurs' tend to stay out of this venture. The macro-entrepreneurs do put notable emphasis on upselling but not by way of the player-driven economies on the platform. The meso- and micro-entrepreneurs operating on the platform place their primary emphasis on initial point of sale in the Steam store. This pattern can partly be explained by conditions outside the platform, such as the wider market order in which the Steam platform is situated, which makes certain actors more significant than others. Moreover, certain mechanisms in digital business models, such as the importance of critical mass to upselling strategies, probably also explain part of the identified pattern. However, the Steam platform also allows us to identify the platform-specific conditions that shape this market order. Valve embraces the modding community and indie developers by making development tools freely available and lowering access barriers to the Steam store, but it also caters to large publishers by reducing its relative share of sales when they pass a certain threshold. It also keeps competitors out of its own key sources of revenue by making these contexts less profitable for other actors on the platform. In this way, the active shaping of market interactions by way of the platform design can be located in the specific conditions associated with different types of economic transactions taking place on the platform. The platform features also enable economic transactions beyond the platform, however, and to get a full picture of the Steam platform economy, it is necessary to include extra-platform activities in the analysis. This will be the subject of the subsequent chapter.

8

Player Trading beyond Steam

In the former chapters, I have analysed and discussed the ways in which the Steam platform has historically expanded the scope of economic transactions (Chapter 5), how this is enabled by the platform features (Chapter 6), and how different actors on the platform turn these affordances into ways of making business (Chapter 7). In this chapter, I will dive deeper into the way these economic transactions extend beyond the Steam platform on to the wider internet. My key point will be that the existence of extra-platform contexts of economic exchange not only serves to expand the number of economic transactions and grow the market, but potentially turns the Steam platform into a payment instrument and skins into a unit of transaction independent of the games from which they originate. Indeed, it can be interpreted as an attempt to create 'money at the margins' (Hütten and Thiemann, 2017) by transforming Steam and its extra-platform transactions into a 'monetary network' (Dodd, 1994). Firstly, I will characterize some of the extra-platform contexts of economic exchange and explain in what way they seem to be 'powered by Steam'. As an extension of this, I will discuss Valve's possible motives for enabling, or at least not policing, these economic practices. These motives can to some degree be tied to the business emphases addressed in Chapter 5, that is, expanding the scope of economic transactions by enabling microtransactions on third-party websites and allowing the secondary market of game items to expand beyond the platform. However, Valve's motives can also be interpreted as an attempt to explore Steam's potential as a social-financial technology beyond its game economies. In the subsequent sections, I will discuss in more detail what this implies. On one hand, the Steam platform does not feature any blockchain technology and does not provide the opportunity of 'mining' for assets. In this way, we are by no means talking about a new kind of cryptocurrency system in the established sense of the word. On the other hand, the avid trading community of Steam gamers can be seen as an alternative and perhaps even more important resource for developing a local medium of exchange which allows players to trade items and engage in economic practices beyond the game economies in which these communities originate, effectively linking the Steam platform to wider economic practices on the internet.

The exchange of game items beyond the Steam platform

A few searches on the internet reveal that the exchange of game items is by no means limited to the context of the Steam community market. In the periphery of the Steam platform exists an abundance of websites that transform the 'money games' (Boluk and LeMieux, 2017) on Steam into various types of business. These websites are, for the most part, rather obscure in terms of their status and purpose, and it is difficult to keep a stable record of them because they incessantly disappear and reappear in new versions, most likely to dodge authorities that block them in an attempt to enforce national gambling regulation. Furthermore, some of these sites are direct scams that are primarily put in place to deprive users of their items without offering them any value in return, that is, direct fraud as opposed to the more conventional and somewhat socially accepted swindle that gambling implicates. Not all of these sites offer gambling, though, and a more systematic examination of the business models emerging in extension of Steam-based player trading discloses a variety of interconnected businesses that transform game items into *goods* that can be bought and sold, *tokens* that can be wagered, *prizes* that can be won, and even *rewards* or *salaries* that can be earned. In combination, these websites make up an alternative and somewhat clandestine ecosystem of businesses that contribute to the Steam platform economy by expanding the total amount of transactions on the platform, but also adding to the more general status of the Steam platform as an economic infrastructure and to game items' status as units of transaction. Before I continue to describe some of these business models, however, I will have to clarify some of the terminology.

In Chapter 5, I discuss skins in relation to the affective value generated in games. Skins are 'cosmetic items', that is, items that do not represent any gameplay advantage yet are still endowed with a huge amount of social prestige. This prestige is rooted in the design of specific game titles and their communities. The skins are typically designed in accordance with tier systems and principles of scarcity, such as 'common', 'rare', and 'epic', or released in limited time periods or on certain occasions that endow them with certain value insofar as a sufficient share of a sufficiently large gamer community choose to 'play along' and attach meaning and value to the game items in accordance with these design choices. It is this 'social and affective labour' of gaming communities that is transformed into market value through the process of 'disembedment' I describe in Chapter 5. The game items that are being traded or gambled on various websites beyond the Steam platform belong to this specific class of virtual items, hence the terms 'skin trading' and 'skin betting'. Moreover, these skins derive from a rather limited group of game titles on the Steam platform, most notably *Counter-Strike: Global Offensive*, *Team Fortress 2* and *Dota 2*, which are all published by Valve, as well as *PlayerUnknown's Battlegrounds* and (on a few occasions) *Rust*, that represent interesting examples of alternative actors apparently turning player trading into a revenue model. Skins and other game items from alternative platforms and game titles may appear depending on whether the website in question is exclusively based on a Steam login or a combination of several platforms. I will return to this question in my subsequent analysis.

A closer examination of the websites that enable the exchange of skins beyond the Steam platform reveals several types of business models and several ways of using Steam as a transaction platform for this purpose. Some websites primarily convey or enable the trading of skins as a *virtual good*. Such websites include cs.money, cs.deals, and skinwallet. Moreover, csgoskins.gg aggregate skins from a multitude of different skin-trading sites. On these websites, different skins and loot boxes are displayed with a price in conventional currencies depending on localization, such as euros, dollars, or Danish kroner. In this way, they basically establish an alternative interface to skin trading on the Steam platform, where skins can also be traded in conventional currencies. When skins are traded directly on the Steam platform, sales are deposited in the Steam Wallet, from which credits cannot be withdrawn, only used for new game titles or game items on the platform: 'funds added to the Steam Wallet are non-refundable and non-transferable. Steam Wallet funds do not constitute a personal property right, have no value outside Steam and can only be used to order Subscriptions and related content via Steam.[1] In comparison, external skin-trading sites, such as the ones previously mentioned, allow users to sell or buy skins using their credit card and bank account, in this way establishing a direct link between skin-trading practices and the wider economic system. As I will return to, this is key to skins' convertibility and potential use as alternative units of transaction.

Other websites integrate skins in direct gambling and betting. This is done by way of 'case-opening' sites and casino sites. On case-opening sites such as csgocases.com, players pay to open loot boxes and get the content. In these cases, skins are treated as 'unknown but potentially valuable virtual goods', and the concept can be seen as an extension of the proliferation of 'mystery boxes' as a general consumption pattern, where consumers pay to receive a box without knowing the contents in advance (see, for instance, hypedrop.com). Whether this represents gambling or not depends on the potential value and fungibility of the content in question. Nielsen and Grabarczyk have suggested a typology focusing on the degree to which players pay for the lootbox in the first place, and whether the reward can be converted into conventional money (2018; Xiao et al, 2021). While most people would agree that a Kinder Surprise egg does not represent an instance of gambling, since the contained items can hardly be traded at a noticeable price, the situation is somewhat different if the box contains an iPhone. In terms of skins, they vary considerably in price, with the majority selling for a few dollars and a few skyrocketing due to a range of reasons. Moreover, they are convertible into conventional currency due to the skin-trading websites mentioned in the previous paragraph. On the traditional casino game websites such as csgoempire.com, skins are included as *prices* that can be *won* and, in many cases, also as *tokens* that can be *wagered* in games such as Coinflip, Roulette, and Blackjack. In these cases, skins effectively take the role that money has in traditional gambling, further enhancing their status as local money and units of transaction.

Finally, a few yet notable websites have included skins as one of the ways users can be compensated for performing different types of 'microwork'. On idleempire.com, users can share data, fill in surveys, watch videos, and so on, basically offering their personal data and eyeballs to various types of business actors in the attention economies of the internet. In compensation, they can earn a range of virtual goods such as gift cards for Amazon and gift cards and items for different games titles, including *Counter-Strike: Global Offensive* and *League of Legends*. As compared to the skin-trading sites mentioned at the beginning of this section, Steam-based game titles appear in concert with a range of alternative game titles and other services on the internet, establishing yet another link to wider economic practices. Thus, even though the websites that compensate microwork with game items do not directly use the Steam platform conducting transactions, their existence is quite significant, since they represent yet another way skins can be transformed into a general unit of transaction, that is, in the form of a *reward* and a *salary*. Technically, these sites do not use Steam as a transaction mechanism, however, and for the same reason, they are not directly linked to trading on Steam in the same way as the skin-trading and skin-betting sites, which are for the most part 'powered by steam, not affiliated with Valve Corp'.

'Powered by Steam, not affiliated with Valve Corp.'

In Chapter 6, I analysed the Steamworks documentation to map how economic interaction and monetary exchanges are enabled by the platform's API. In this process, I identified a few ways that Steam differs from other digital entertainment platforms. One key characteristic is the denunciation of advertising as a revenue model and, conversely, the prominence of microtransactions as an alternative. The Steamworks documentation clearly expresses that no limits are placed on the way individual publishers choose to integrate this feature in their gameplay, as long as they use it:

> Steam places no restrictions on what you sell or how you sell it, nor does it preclude the use of whatever other mechanisms your game has for selling items. Its purpose is to bring a common payment experience that user's (sic) are familiar with from the Steam platform into your game and allow them to easily spend their Steam wallet value on your products.[2]

This indicates that microtransactions represent a key business emphasis from the perspective of the platform owner. This can also be detected from the degree to which the microtransaction system is integrated with other functionalities on the platform. The microtransaction system and the consequent use of the Steam Wallet can be integrated into the games themselves, the Steam workshop, and the community market, and the Steamworks documentation also provides an implementation guide for publishers who would like to integrate the microtransaction system on an external web page. The latter is quite notable, since this part of the Steamworks documentation directly incites economic actors to perform transactions beyond the level of the platform. Importantly, this possibility of performing microtransactions beyond the level of the Steam platform does not enable the skin-betting practices I describe in the previous section. The microtransaction system primarily allows publishers to sell game items to their players using the Steam Wallet, no matter if this takes place in the game, in the Steam-based inventory store, or from the game's web page beyond the platform. To set up a service where players can buy skins from other gamers and sell or wager their own skins, the service provider must be able to exchange skins on the Steam platform on behalf of these players. This option is not available in the microtransaction API, so to be able to perform this action, trading sites either facilitate direct transactions between players exchanging skins on their websites, or use a trade bot. The trade bot solution is most likely also the method that is put to use on the skin-gambling sites. In practice, this is done by asking the user to log in with their Steam account and to share their trade URL. On skin-trading sites that enable direct transaction between players, sellers will also have to accept the trade once it has been set up. On skin-trading sites using trade bots, the seller deposits their skins on to the site when they list their items. Skin trading based on direct transactions between players is an advantage for sellers, who will not have to deposit their items before they can be listed; skin trading using trade bots is an advantage for buyers, who can pick up their items as soon as they have paid for them, without waiting for the seller to accept the trade on the Steam platform. Obviously, this is a less straightforward and considerably more dodgy way of integrating the Steam platform functionalities into extra-platform economic practices. Several web pages state that they are 'powered by Steam, not Affiliated with Valve corp.', and Valve does seem to place certain limits on it. In the face of rising public concern over the economic practices emerging in relation to the Steam platform, Valve introduced a 'cooldown' in 2018, which implied that skins could only be resold seven days after they had been acquired on the platform. Similarly, it takes seven days from when a new account has been opened to buy trade skins in the Steam community market. Moreover, Steam does seem to monitor and close accounts associated with scams, though gambling is not mentioned directly in the trading policy and recommended trading practices.[3] Nevertheless, available estimates do indicate that skin betting represents a thriving business, and it is worth considering the degree to which Valve has strategic interest in Steam being used for this purpose.[4]

Steam's economic interests in extra-platform practices

Depending on the specific ways different actors make use of Steam as a platform for transaction, Valve earns a share. Whenever a microtransaction takes place by way of the microtransaction system, Valve earns 30 per cent, no matter if this takes place in the game, in an item shop, or on an external website. In this way, authorized uses of the microtransaction system are clearly in Valve's interest. Moreover, the use of Steam gift cards and skins as compensation for microwork on various GPT sites represents a direct business interest for Steam because it figures as additional sales. Whether the skin-trading and skin-gambling sites mentioned in the previous section represent a direct revenue for Valve or not depends on whether they are based on direct exchanges between players using the inventory-based trading option or whether they make use of the Steam community market. In the first case, no direct economic exchange takes place of which Valve can earn a share; in the second, Valve will earn 5 per cent of every trade taking place, plus an additional 10 per cent 'game fee' if items derive from *Counter-Strike: Global Offensive*, *Dota 2*, *Team Fortress 2*, or *Artifact*, which are all published by Valve.[5] In this scenario, skin-betting and skin-trading sites can be considered a direct extension of Valve's current business model on Steam.

Though it is hard to confirm directly, the skin-trading and skin-gambling sites addressed in this chapter most likely make use of the inventory-based trading option, of which Valve earns no share. Indeed, third-party skin-trading websites effectively deprive Valve of the revenue it could have earned if these skins had been traded in the Steam community market. Yet, even if Valve does not earn a direct share of the exchanges taking place on skin-trading and skin-gambling sites, they do represent an advantage in the wider Steam platform economy. The indirect facilitation of skin-trading and skin-gambling practices beyond the platform can be interpreted as a strategic attempt to grow the market, stimulate the demand for more skins, and regulate prices (Thorhauge and Nielsen, 2021). That is, while Steam may not earn a share of every exchange taking place beyond the level of the platform, enabling a secondary market is a common approach to growing an existing market. Lehdonvirta and Castronova (2014) explain Amazon's strategic interests in enabling secondary trade on the 'Amazon marketplace' as a trade-off between the risk of cannibalizing the existing market on one hand and the chance of expanding the existing market on the other, since the same items can be sold on several occasions (2014: 92–3). The Steam community market can similarly be defined as a secondary market context growing the general market for skins. Valve does have a direct interest in keeping secondary trade to its own marketplace, where the corporation earns a share of every trade; however, trades taking place beyond the platform certainly represent a strategic interest too, even if Valve does not earn a share. This is the case because these contexts of economic exchange also serve to grow the general market and, hence, the demand for skins on the Steam platform and, as an extension of this, the pricing of skins (Thorhauge and Nielsen, 2021; see also Zanescu et al, 2020). In this way, the relatively half-hearted attempt at regulating the exchange of skins beyond the level of the platform may be due to these activities being pretty much in line with Steam's general business model. Finally, the enabling of extra-platform economic transactions can be interpreted as a way of 'expanding diagonally' (Doyle, 2013) into the field of financial technology. It is notorious that Valve itself defines its platform as a 'payment method' in the Steamworks documentation[6] when explaining how to use the microtransaction system on an external website. In the subsequent section, I will explore in more detail the notion of monetary networks as an analytical perspective on the ecosystem of websites enabling the exchange of skins beyond the Steam platform and the transformation of gaming communities into 'transactional communities' (Schwartz, 2020).

Monetary networks and money at the margins

With reference to Schumpeter, Ingham (2013) identifies two historical approaches to money: the commodity theory and the claim theory. From the perspective of the former, money is basically just another type of commodity, which differs from other commodities due to its interchangeability. In contrast, the claim theory focuses on a more abstract notion of money as 'money of account', that is, money as a phenomenon that consists of claims and credits (Ingham: 21). It is by way of the latter that the phenomenon of 'credit money' has become the most dominating form in late capitalism, where the creation of money is directly tied to the creation of debt (Dodd,

2018). According to Ingham, and contrary to popular beliefs that primitive commodity money has 'evolved' into money of account, money 'is always an abstract claim or credit whose "moneyness" is conferred by money of account' (2013: 49). Even in ancient Babylon, commodity money was backed by a system of account, supported by a local political authority. Dodd criticizes this emphasis on state and sovereignty in the definition of money and points out that it 'reduces money to state-issued currency' (2005). He emphasizes the 'diversification of money', including local forms of money that are not necessarily issued by a state or political authority. What both Ingham and Dodd have in common, though, is a focus on the 'production of money' as key to the analysis of money as a phenomenon. Ingham points out that much of classic economic theory builds on the idea that money is a neutral commodity, a 'veil' that covers what can basically be boiled down to a barter economy (Samuelson, 1974, cited in Ingham, 2004). In doing so, economic theory fails to explain and take into consideration the way money is created and distributed in society. He points out that power in societies not only relates to possession and quantities of money but also to who can *produce* money in the first place, with the state and the banking system as key institutions in question. Dodd, in comparison, emphasizes 'the network of social relationship that make [economic] transactions possible' rather than the object exchanged or the exchange relationship itself (1994: xxiii), and sets out to define relevant analytical perspectives on this network. This focus on money as a phenomenon that exists in networks is also predominant in Lana Schwartz's account of how 'payment became social media' (2020). Though her emphasis is primarily on payment technologies and how Big Tech is diversifying into this domain (see Chapter 8), her understanding of money as a communicative phenomenon and her concept of 'transactional communities' (2020: 16) provides a more detailed account of the 'networks of social relationships' Dodd may be pointing to, beyond the notions of geographical territories and nation states, emphasizing the shared identity, geography, temporality, value, politics, and practices (2020: 18). All of these approaches are useful for understanding the cornucopia of monetary phenomena that have emerged on the internet during the last decade, such as Bitcoin and cryptocurrencies.

Bitcoin has been explained as 'commodity money without gold, fiat money without state and credit money without debt' (Bjerg, 2016), and can, in this way, be defined through a double disintermediation from the bank and states (Dodd, 2018), the two key institutions in Ingham's definition of money. Technically, this is done by replacing the authority of the state and the money-lending power of the bank with the 'distributed ledger' made possible by blockchain technologies. This double disintermediation is tied to the 'tech-utopian' idea that Bitcoin can 'remove politics from the production and management of money altogether' (2018: 8). However, as

Dodd points out, this is an illusion, since Bitcoin relies on a great deal of social organization. Indeed, the overwhelming focus on the algorithmic aspects of cryptocurrencies has overshadowed the social, institutional, and political processes, and indeed the transactional communities, that are involved in their creation and maintenance. For instance, Hütten and Thiemann define Bitcoin as a 'money game' and describe its relation vis-à-vis other monetary systems and legal frameworks as a historic development from confrontation to horizontal and vertical integration with wider economic systems (2017). This development has ensured Bitcoin a place 'at the margins' of the global monetary system by 'weaving itself into the dominant money games' (2017: 25). Similarly, Lana Schwartz's notion of 'transactional communities' makes obvious the many ways in which money and payment are deeply intertwined with social interaction and identities. Accordingly, while the surge of cryptocurrencies has led us to consider blockchains to be an indispensable feature, their status as money has less to do with their specific programmed properties and more to do with general institutional and political rearrangements, that is, a 'reorganization of the monetary networks' in Dodd's terms, and the transformation of gaming communites into transactional communites in Schwartz's terms.

The skin ecosystem as a monetary network

Dodd's notion of 'monetary networks' has not gained a lot of ground since he introduced the term in 1994. Yet, this concept is very useful in the context of the present analysis because it allows us to reduce states and banks to variables rather than constitutive actors in the production of money, while avoiding, on the other hand, reducing money to its physical or programmed properties, such as blockchain technologies. Dodd's (1994) definition of monetary networks in 1994 includes:

1. a standardized accounting system;
2. information about temporal characteristics, that is, the expectation that money can still be used in the future;
3. information about the spatial characteristics, that is, the territory within which the money can be used;
4. legalistic information, usually in the form of rules; and
5. knowledge of the behaviour and expectations of others.

As concerns the standardized accounting system, this is what is ensured by the intermediation of states and banks in Ingham's approach to monetary systems, and what is allegedly done by blockchain technologies in the case of Bitcoin, though Dodd adeptly demonstrates that even in the case of Bitcoin, it is trust rather than the technological system itself that does the job (2018). In terms of skins, the standardized accounting systems are partly handled by the Steam platform and partly by the skin-trading sites analysed previously. The Steam platform offers a transaction mechanism (Lehdonvirta and Castronova, 2014) and an inventory service that allows players to exchange skins, and keeps track of who 'owns' a skin at a certain point in time (I use quotation marks here because the skins are in principle the property of the platform; see Joseph, 2021). Moreover, the skin-trading sites provide convertibility of skins into conventional currencies so that their value can be accounted for in terms of the currencies into which they are convertible, in this way 'piggy bagging' the wider monetary systems, as observed by Hütten and Thiemann, 2017 in the case of Bitcoin.

As concerns information about money's temporal and spatial characteristics, this is traditionally tied to national or regional territories and the anticipation that they will persist in the future. However, as Lana Schwartz points out in her analysis of the way 'payment became social media' (2020), payment creates a shared social world or 'transaction community' defined as 'the set of relations that are produced by transaction communication' (2020: 16), which does not only concern national territory but 'imbricated senses of identity, geography, temporality, value, politics and practice' (2020: 18). In the case of Bitcoin and player-driven economies, which are not tied to a specific national territory, it is rather the relative size, extension, and nature of the phenomenon on the internet that informs the expectations of potential users and the identifies, values, politics, and practices shared in specific gaming communities. As early as 2001, Castronova pointed out that the in-game currency of the MMORPG *Everquest* had better exchange rates than those of several national currencies (2008). A similar example is *World of Warcraft*, which allowed players to buy items from non-player characters for gold, and in later iterations, players could also trade items in between them in designated auction houses, using in-game gold as a standard. This turned trading in *World of Warcraft* into a metagame in its own right and spawned a thriving business at the borders of the game, where 'gold farmers' played the game to collect gold and resell it for dollars, euros, or yen. Exchange rate does not make a currency alone, of course, but the size and the extension of the phenomenon does provide relevant information about its spatial and temporal properties, such as whether a certain type of money can be used in specific contexts and whether it is likely to be valid in the future. Thus, enabling the exchange of skins beyond the Steam platform is basically allowing the economic practices to extend in space and time to stabilize the monetary network. The bigger the monetary network is, the larger the applicability of the unit of transaction in space and time.

As concerns 'legalistic information in the form of rules', Nigel Dodd most likely refers to those legal frameworks that regulate economic transactions in national contexts, or in the terminology of Fligstein, the rules of transaction

(Fligstein, 1996, 2001). These have a limited presence in the contexts of skin trading and skin gambling, where warnings of scams and fraud abound, among other reasons because the distributed and obscure character of the practice makes it difficult to establish which legal frameworks should be applied and how they should be enforced. However, the platform's features represent a regulatory alternative. Indeed, this is a very straightforward example of the way 'code is law' (Lessig, 2006) in the context of platform markets. Just like Steam shapes market interactions on the platform by way of its design (see Chapter 6), it shapes transactions beyond the platform by making certain actions, such as the exchange of skins, possible, while at the same time imposing limits on these actions, such as whether and when certain skins can be traded. While Valve may assert that the corporation is not involved with the economic practices of skin trading and skin gambling taking place beyond the Steam platform (and certainly has clear legal interest in maintaining this claim), the practices are still enabled and directly governed by the platform design – 'powered by Steam, not affiliated with Valve corp'. Specific changes in the platform features, such as the 2018 cooldown, directly affect economic practices beyond the platform and the features can in this way be considered a sort of indirect, automated governance.

Finally, Nigel Dodd includes knowledge of the behaviour and expectations of others as a key dimension of monetary networks and points out that this information is 'vital in generating trust in money's abstract properties' (1994). Indeed, trust represents a key issue in the literature on money, as the acceptance of certain symbolic artefacts as representations of value requires a high level of trust ('fiat money' literally translates into 'trust money'). Trust is also a key issue in research on online interaction in market contexts and beyond because the lack of physical and non-verbal cues in any sort of online interaction represents a challenge to the establishment of trust between actors. A range of systems have been put in place to make up for this lack of information, such as the use of services like Trustpilot. For instance, csgoskins.gg, an aggregator of skin-trading sites, uses 'community ratings' from Trustpilot as an indicator of a site's trustworthiness.[7] In this way, skin trading and skin gambling face the same types of trust issues as other contexts of transaction on the internet, and look towards the same types of solutions. It is worth noting, though, that trust as a stabilizing factor in monetary networks has more than one dimension. It may relate to the specific contexts or actors of exchange, and it may relate to the general acceptance of certain objects' status as money or representation of value. 'We accept money ... because we have a sense that institutions authorize it ... who else will accept it' (Schwartz, 2020). The first dimension is addressed through services such as Trustpilot, while the second is a much more abstract and distributed phenomenon that is traditionally tied to the institutional role of central banks and national authorities (Ingham, 2013), yet it can historically be tied to a much broader range of political projects and utopias (Eich, 2019). In the case of skins as a potential unit of transaction, this trust is upheld by the gaming community as a transactional community. Indeed, the core members of the Steam community, who celebrate the platform as morally superior to its competitors and Gabe Newell, Valve's CEO, as their moral leader, are another key component in the creation of general trust in the 'utopia of skins'.

Does this mean that skins represent a new type of game-based money and with a transactional community of gamers? Yes and no. Indeed, the vagueness of this answer may be the whole point. According to 'Goodhart's law', as soon as a particular instrument or asset is publicly defined as money in order to be controlled, that asset ceases to be used as money because substitutes will be produced for purposes of evasion' (Dodd, 2018: xx). Valve may have an interest in skins being used as money and as investment assets, while avoiding naming them as such for purposes of evasion. While Bitcoin was launched with a manifesto defining it as a new, revolutionary currency that directly confronted the prevailing system (Hütten and Thiemann, 2017), skins as a monetary network rather seem to flourish in a grey zone between sanctioned and non-sanctioned economic transactions (powered by Steam, not affiliated with Valve Corp.), at the intersections between player-driven economies and the wider internet and between money and non-money. They can meaningfully be defined as a monetary network where key aspects, such as the standardized accounting system, is ensured through its relationship with other economic practices on the internet, while they do not represent a stable, self-contained currency (if there ever was one). Rather, the Steam platform design and Valve's offhand approach to the manifold uses of it enhance skins 'moneyness' and allows it to unfold as a living experiment at the margins of the conventional monetary system.

To sum up, a range of third-party websites use the Steam platform's trading affordances to integrate skins, cosmetic game items, into a range of economic practices. The skins effectively take the role of money in these contexts, where they are used as wagers, prizes, and rewards. Thus, the Steam platform, third-party websites, and the practices they support can be analysed as a monetary network, that is, a 'network of social relationships that make [economic] transactions possible' (Dodd, 1994: xxiii). This does not necessarily turn skins into a fully fledged currency; Valve Corporation and the third-party actors involved may even have a strategic interest in keeping them under the radar of various legal frameworks associated with the regulation of currencies. But the existence of this network bears witness to several important aspects of the Steam platform's tangled market. First of all, the tangled market of Steam extends well beyond the platform and should not be considered something that is confined to the platform itself. The study of platforms as tangled markets should also include how key features are put to use in a range of alternative contexts beyond the platform. Moreover, even though these extra-platform practices are 'not affiliated with Valve Corporation', they do help expand the scope of economic transactions by raising the demand for skins (Thorhauge and Nielsen, 2021) and growing the market in general. Finally, these extra-platform market contexts take the form of emerging practices upheld by inventive actors and avid trading communities on and beyond the platform, who engage in economic action in accordance with their own interest while, at the same time, they generate value for the platform. This, somewhat counterintuitively, turns trade into an alternative kind of immaterial labour (Terranova, 2003). While the notion of user commodification on digital platforms primarily deals with the user as consumer or prosumer (Manzerolle, 2010; Fuchs, 2013; Nieborg, 2016), the trader may represent an alternative version of the user commodity, which requires us to reconsider the notion of commodification in relation to the production, consumption, and economic exchange of content on digital platforms. This will be the subject of Chapter 9.

User Monetization and Value Creation in Tangled Markets

In this concluding chapter, I will discuss how user commodification is expanded and intensified in tangled markets and how this development challenges current approaches to the regulation of platforms. Since Smythe's seminal work on the 'audience commodity' (1981), the role of advertising has been a key focus in the conceptualization of commodification processes in commercial media, and it remains an important backdrop to widely used concepts such as 'the attention economy' (Goldhaber, 1997) and 'the marketplace of attention' (Webster, 2014). Of course, advertising as a business model has been expanded throughout this history and commodification has been intensified through mechanisms of datafication (Van Dijck et al, 2018: 37) and a gradual shift from attention to engagement as a key focus of this commodification (Ørmen and Gregersen, 2022). As the previous chapters indicate, advertising is by no means the only way in which users are monetized and commodified on digital platforms and the specific approach employed by Valve on the Steam platform allows us to consider in more detail alternatives beyond advertising. On Steam, users are also addressed as traders that create value for the platform by way of their economic action. This business model, more specifically, consists in converting the value players attach to their game worlds into market value through the integration of transactional affordances into a range of contexts on the platform (see Chapter 5). In this way, the core of Steam's business model is not the audience commodity but rather the commodification of player-driven economies.

In this chapter, I will argue that existing approaches to audience and user commodification in the context of digital media primarily position users as consumers, though the category of consumer is extended in a range of ways. In response to this, I will suggest that all steps in the process, from production over exchange to consumption, have been commodified in the context of Steam's tangled markets. Users may participate as consumers, producers, or traders and still be commodified in this platform business model. In the subsequent sections of this chapter, I will firstly track the concept of commodification and the audience commodity historically, and how this concept and line of thought has extended into digital communication environments. As an extension of this, I will discuss how insights from the analysis of Steam's tangled markets may inform our understanding of the user not primarily as consumer but as consumer, producer, and trader. Finally, I will address how this approach to commodifying users is by no means limited to the contexts of Steam and the domain of gaming, even though it may take a very specific shape in the context of Steam. Indeed, digital platforms are currently diversifying into the domains of personal finance and peer-to-peer transactions, and new platforms are appearing that place their primary focus on users as financial traders. This brings new perspectives to commodification, including the potential commodification of a wide range of domains in everyday life, and challenges current regulatory frameworks and their occupation with personal data.

Commodification and the audience commodity

In my introduction to Polanyi's historical account of the market society, I put forward his notion of fictitious commodities (see Chapter 3). Fictious commodities differ from ordinary commodities in having been created for other purposes, with land, labour, and money as key examples. For instance, people don't have children with the purpose of supplying the production chain; nevertheless, they are turned into 'fictitious commodities' in the form of labour power in industrial societies. Though his inclusion of money into this category is somewhat curious, the notion of fictitious commodities corresponds well with more recent approaches of commodification. In the 1970s, the concept of commodification was used simultaneously in art and literary studies, world system theory, and Marxist welfare state literature (Hermann, 2021: 2). In art and literary studies, the focus was on the implications of the commodity form to the field of art, drawing on Adorno and Horkheimer's critical writings on the culture industry (1972 [1947]). Within this framework, commodification was seen as a counterforce to the liberating potential of mass media, ultimately leading to mass consumption rather than general enlightenment.[1] In world system theory and Marxist welfare state literature, the concept was used to describe the shift from feudalism to capitalism, the commodification of land and labour, and the welfare state's counterstrategy of 'decommodification' (Hermann, 2021: 3), such as the work of Wallerstein (1983). While Polanyi is not cited directly in these sources, the world system theory and the welfare state literature's use of the term correspond well with Polanyi's concepts of embeddedness and fictitious commodities addressed in Chapter 3.

A highly influential publication in the context of media studies is Dallas W. Smythe's chapter 'On the audience commodity and its work' in his book *Dependency Road* published in 1981 (Smythe, 1981). In this chapter, Smythe launches the somewhat provocative idea that the audience is what is being bought and sold in commercial media. The conventional understanding of advertisement-based media involves that editorial content represents the primary content and purpose of mass media, and advertising purely enables this content economically. Smythe oppositely points out that the actual product of commercial media is the audience, which is packaged and sold to advertisers (Smythe, 1981: 233). This argument entails a chain of equally provocative statements that are still highly pertinent today. One is that the distinction between editorial content and advertising is an illusion. 'The fiction that the advertising supports or makes possible the news, entertainment, or "educational" content has been a public relations mainstay of the commercial media', Smythe writes; in practice, the purpose of editorial content is to '(1) attract and keep [the audience] attending to the program, newspaper, or magazine; (2) cultivate a mood conducive to favorable reaction to the advertisers' explicit and implicit messages' (1981b: 241–2). While media studies at the time (and today) would generally consider editorial content to be the primary content of commercial media, Smythe argues that advertising is in practice the primary content.

This critique has been influential in classic media studies and remains important to research in the field of cultural production on digital platforms today. For instance, much of YouTube's business concerns the strategic alignment of major brands and key content creators to ensure 'brand-safe content' (Ørmen and Gregersen, 2022). Similarly, Manzerolle and Daubs address how social media influencers 'build trust and then leverage that trust in services of commercial messages' (2021: 1285). Another provocative statement is the idea that the audience's activity of attending commercial media can be considered a form of work: 'The work which audience members perform for the advertiser to whom they have been sold is learning to buy goods and to spend their income accordingly' (Smythe, 1981: 243). This runs somewhat counter to common notions of work and productivity, and Smythe puts considerable effort into arguing that this is actually the case. Yet, in the field of consumption studies, the overlap between consumption and production is described at length (Ritzer and Jurgenson, 2010), and the notion of immaterial labour is a key theme in Marxist analyses of user exploitation on the internet (Terranova, 2000). Manzerolle adds to these notions of immaterial labour that of active 'self-commodification', which happens when 'one's self-reflexive and social capacities are increasingly inseparable from the machinations of capital accumulation and capital intensive ICT infrastructure, which are increasingly central to the articulation and deployment of one's personal capacities' (2010: 459). Accordingly, the users' active participation and content creation at the beginning of the millennium celebrated as an empowerment of users can also be seen as the opposite, an expansion of audience work in Smythe's sense of the concept, submitting the subjective experience, personal expression, and social connectivity to the interests of brands and advertisers. From this perspective, players' active transformation of games as programmed systems into meaningful interaction and the value they attach to the game world in the process is simultaneously play and labour – 'in play labour, joy and play become toil and work, and toil and work appear to be joy and play' (Fuchs, 2013: 60) – or playbour (Kücklich, 2005), and lies at the core of Valve's business model on Steam (see Chapter 5).

As concerns the logics of advertising, digital media do not represent a disruption from traditional mass media but rather an acceleration and augmentation of a business logic already present in the 'consciousness industries' (Smythe, 1981). While the notion of surveillance capitalism (Zuboff, 2019) may indicate a change from earlier forms of capitalism, the basic logic of monetization remains the same. The key development concerns the level of granularity of this segmentation as well as the data that informs it, which has changed from crude demographic and sociographic categories to various types of metadata, location data, and use data created by the users themselves as they use the internet: 'Commodification is intensified by mechanisms of datafication as the massive amount of user data collected and processed by online platforms provide into users' interests and needs at a particular point in time' (Van Dijck et al, 2018: 37). Moreover, the scope of datafication has been extended to 'commodify individuals as audiences (to advertisers), as fans (to content creators) and as consumers (to brands)' (Ørmen and Gregersen, 2022: 4), in this way intensifying the process of commodification. The impact and range of advertising as a business model is so large that it is sometimes directly included as one of the constituencies of platforms and platform logics. For instance, Gillespie, in his work on platforms as politics, states that the 'business of being a cultural intermediary is a complex and fragile one, oriented as it is to at least three constituencies: end users, advertisers and professional content producers' (2010: 353). Similarly, Burgess points out that platform logics shape what counts as value and convert those measurements into semi-automated decisions about what is pushed to audiences and the extent to which that content can attract advertising value (2021: 23). Nevertheless, this is not the only form of audience monetization, and a range of emerging and established business models within digital platforms, such as subscription-based streaming services, represent alternative (though not necessarily new) frameworks for user monetization that do not fit the categories of advertising or audience commodities very well.

The audience commodity and audience work in tangled markets

While the advertising business model prevails on digital platforms, it is not the only one. Several alternative approaches, including Steam's 'tangled markets', call for a reconsideration of the ways in which users are monetized and commodified on digital platforms. The 'audience commodity' is still a somewhat adequate designation of what is being sold in Facebook's advertising market, even though the scope of datafication has been extended (Ørmen and Gregersen, 2022) and serves a broader range of purposes in commercial media. If we turn our attention toward subscription-based games and streaming services, the audience commodity becomes a somewhat less precise designation of the business model in question. While the detailed tracking of audiences is certainly key to this business model as well, the purpose of tracking is not exactly the production of an audience commodity, it is rather the strategic alignment of content and audiences in ways that ensure continued use and thus monthly payments. Once we turn our attention to the marketplaces enabled by digital platforms, the notion of the audience commodity stops being meaningful, and we need a different terminology for addressing the type of work and commodification processes this involves. I will suggest an alternative framework, distinguishing analytically between the positions of the consumer, the producer, and the trader.

As I will also return to by the end of this chapter, digital platforms are currently integrating transactional affordances in a range of ways. Manzerolle and Wiseman point to the way transactional ecosystems of commerce and attention (2016: 395) are converging on contemporary platforms, and in a later publication, Manzerolle and Daubs define this development as an effort to 'link advertising and point-of-purchase' (2021: 1281) directly on platforms, addressing users simultaneously as audiences and consumers. Ørmen and Gregersen similarly address how users are simultaneously analysed and commodified as audiences, consumers, and fans in the contexts of YouTube's business models (2022). This development changes the nature of 'the audience commodity' on digital platforms by establishing a direct link between it and the consumer, basically turning the two into one. That is, users are not just addressed and measured as 'potential consumers' but also as consumers per se in the evolving business models of digital platforms. This does not make the notion of the audience commodity irrelevant, though; the development indicated by Manzerolle et al and Schwartz will very likely further augment and intensify the trading of user attention now enriched with transactional data representing the 'perhaps most crucial type of meta-data since they reflect actual, rather than assumed, behaviour' (Manzerolle and Wiseman, 2016: 401). Hence, this rather leads to a new concept of the 'consumer commodity' who simultaneously pays with money and attention on digital platforms.

Within the domain of gaming, the changing role of the 'audience commodity' has been addressed by David Nieborg (2015) in his work on the free-to-play game as a connective commodity. He analyses how business models of digital platforms frame the design and business models of entrepreneurs offering cultural products on these platforms, with *Candy Crush Saga* across the App Store, Facebook, and Google Play as his primary case. He argues that 'the rules of play for game apps are as much governed by a game's ludic properties as they are structured and alternated by a market logic which is mutually constituted by the connective logic of social media platforms' (2015: 1–2). That is, the business strategies of complementors on digital platforms, as I also demonstrate in my analysis of market actors on the Steam platform, are shaped by the affordances of the platform design. As an extension of this line of thought, Nieborg argues that *Candy Crush Saga* comprises a number of different revenue models that can be summarized into in-app purchases, virality, and advertising involving different types of commodities: the product commodity, the prosumer commodity, and the player commodity. While the first of these commodities points to the option of buying additional content, meaning that the content itself is the commodity, the second concerns 'how the connective affordances of Facebook are implemented into the core design of the Saga template' (2015: 8), for instance, by way of 'invitation and gifting mechanics' that incite players to involve their wider Facebook networks (see the section on business models in Chapter 2). In this way, users are in principle turned into unpaid marketing employees. The player commodity, finally, points to the traditional model of advertising, except that it is the player that is commodified, hence 'player commodity'. Moreover, as Manzerolle and Daubs (2021) and Ørmen and Gregersen (2022) also point out, the affordances of digital platforms allow advertisers to link directly to the products that are being advertised.

The revenue models in Nieborg's analysis of *Candy Crush Saga* addresses the player as consumer, as an extended version of the audience commodity, and as prosumer. The latter points to the productive aspects of the act of consumption, which has been addressed extensively in the field of consumption studies (Ritzer and Jurgenson, 2010) and Marxist studies of digital media and the internet (Terranova, 2003; Fuchs, 2021), sometimes referred to as 'prosumption'. This notion of the prosumer certainly addresses productive aspects of consumption on the internet, but it also ties users' productivity firmly to the act of consumption and thus does not capture other productive activities such as the 'playbour' of modders (Kücklich, 2005) or the 'digital dispossession' of user-generated content (Joseph, 2018). Nor does it capture sufficiently the monetizing of users as economic actors on the Steam platform. While the productivity of the prosumer involves the generation of data that platforms use to further personalize advertising (Fuchs, 2013), it does not cover to the same degree the productive practices of creators on social media (Duffy et al, 2019; Baym, 2021) or the productivity of modding communities (Kücklich, 2005; Postigo, 2007; Banks, 2013; Joseph, 2018). Or, at least, it may not be analytically meaningful to categorize these different types of productivity within in the same category of 'prosumption'. Moreover, none of these approaches address the economic action of users as a source of profit, that is, as a user activity generating value for the platform owner.

On the Steam platform, users are monetized in a range of ways, of which some map well on to the suggested terminologies, while others do not. Firstly, players are addressed as consumers in the form of paying customers. In this way, Steam is still, to a large extent, a storefront competing with other storefronts based on a classic retail model, though economic transactions are increasingly extended into the games by way of microtransaction systems (see the section on business models in Chapter 2). In these contexts, the user participates in the role of the consumer. Furthermore, even though the Steam platform does not offer complementors a system for creating advertising revenues in the same way as Facebook or Google Play, players are addressed as 'player commodities' in terms of the platform's own strategic suggestions through various banners, notifications, and the recommendation system. In this way, the 'audience commodity', here transformed into a 'player commodity' (Nieborg, 2015), is still at work in the context of Steam. Similarly, the notion of prosumption makes sense in relation to a wide range of data and content players either passively or actively deliver to the platform. Among the passive, players' purchases and play patterns contribute to the recommendation system, in this way enhancing the platform's strategic alignment of content with player segments. In addition to this, players' participation in game forums and community events serve to consolidate the key asset of the Steam platform: its gaming communities. Indeed, as I argue in Chapter 5, gameplay itself can be considered a distinct form of 'prosumption' generating the affective intensities (Jarett, 2016) and emotional capital (Arvidsson, 2006) of gaming communities that can be converted into market value. In addition to this comes reviews and guides for other players and the creation of additional game items in the Steam workshop.

However, somewhere down the line, these activities increasingly take the form of 'regular productivity' organized in production communities such as modding on Steam (Joseph, 2018). In the Steam community workshop, users may produce additional content and sell it to other users, and in these situations, 'production' becomes a more precise designation than 'prosumption'. Moreover, none of the existing frameworks really cover players' active participation in fictive and real economies as part of the Steam platform's business model. Of course, the purchase of items in the Steam community market and community workshop can be defined as another act of consumption, yet players acting simultaneously as buyers and sellers, constituting 'transactional communities' (Schwartz, 2020), on the platform fit badly into this category. It is necessary to look beyond the categories of consumption and prosumption. I suggest approaching every step of the process – production, trade, and consumption – as a commodified process in the context of tangled markets. Instead of expanding to an unreasonable extent the concept of consumption or prosumption, I suggest that users participate as consumers, producers, and traders in platform economies in ways that generate value for the platform owner. In the terminology of Polanyi, users' acts of consumption, production, and trade are turned into 'fictitious commodities' in the sense that they are accomplished for other reasons, yet are shaped and repurposed to serve the economic interest of the platform owner. Obviously, these activities overlap to a considerable degree and the notion of the prosumer remains meaningful in a wide range of contexts. In this way, the categories of consumer commodity, producer commodity, and trader commodity should be seen as analytical rather than empirical. Production, trade, and consumption overlap in a range of ways, and just like the notion of the prosumer remains a meaningful category, the idea of the 'protrader' may turn out to be useful in the future media environment.

The commodification of users as consumers has been theorized extensively, as the initial sections of this chapter indicate. Moreover, the role of users as producers has received considerable scholarly attention within the field of platform practices and creator cultures (Duffy et al, 2019; Baym, 2021). In comparison, the role of the user as trader and economic actor is relatively non-described. While my analysis of the Steam platform business model gives one specific explanation of the way player-driven economies are transformed into market value, this most likely depends on the specific configuration of the platform. For instance, Steam and Airbnb differ considerably with regard to the way trading is configured and how 'fictitious commodities' are generated. Though not accounting for such differences, it does point to a range of blind spots in current platform studies' approaches to value creation and commodification in platform business models.

Commodification mechanisms, according to Van Dijck et al, are simultaneously empowering and disempowering, 'especially platforms we have labelled as connectors allow, on the one hand, individuals to market their personal assets ... on the other hand the same mechanisms of commodification involve ... the exploitation of cultural labour, the (immaterial) labour of users, and the further precarization of on-demand service workers' (2018: 37). By introducing the opposing notions of empowerment and disempowerment, they point to the fact that processes of commodification often involve the active participation of users that seek their own (economic) interests, while they also exploit the same users in a range of ways. Jarrett similarly notes how our participation in social media is 'both a rewarding moment of socialisation and an instance of exploited labour' (2016: 113), and Manzerolle points to users' active self-commodification in which 'one's self-reflexive and social capacities are increasingly inseparable from the machinations of capital accumulation' (2010). These authors address how users may consider their participation to be entirely in line with their own interests, while they are simultaneously being exploited. Indeed, the empowerment of users through processes of commodification *is* an integration of the self-reflexive and social capacities into the machinations of capital accumulation. Dealing with this contradiction between users' possible experience of empowerment while their actions are being exploited in a number of ways cannot be done without addressing the ideological underpinnings of the entire discussion. Indeed, this contradiction marks the historical line that goes between the Frankfurt school tradition of the 1960s and the cultural studies tradition of the 1970s and 1980s, and remains a point of controversy today. What is different is the gradual change of perspective from audiences and consumers to a range of roles and identities that do not fit as neatly into the notion of the commodity, which, after all, connotates passivity. These roles include players, traders, and micro-entrepreneurs, who are not just active participants but often participate in ways that are associated with the role of the 'capitalist', such as trading, speculating in financial assets, and extracting surplus value in the process. Indeed, while the challenge of cultural studies throughout the 1970s and 1980s was to convince the world that the seemingly passive undertaking of watching television and consuming goods was an active accomplishment (for example, Stuart Hall, 1980), the challenge today is rather to understand in depth the ways in which economic action on digital platforms can in fact be commodified to the same extent as audiences and consumers.

Concluding remarks: the platformization of peer-to-peer transactions and the regulation of tangled markets

In her introduction to the platformization of peer-to-peer transactions or 'how payment became social media', Lana Schwartz asks 'what happens when Silicon Valley behemoths turn their attention to money' (2020: 2). In her book, Schwartz adeptly demonstrates how payment technologies across all ages have shaped money and monetary practices, and how social media platforms' current inroads into peer-to-peer transactions are changing money once again. While large platforms such as YouTube, Facebook, and Instagram have primarily based their business models on advertising, a range of recent developments indicate that their interests in various types of financial technologies and associated business models are increasing, such as Facebook's attempt to launch its own cryptocurrency (Schwartz, 2020), Instagram's integration of transactional affordances (Manzerolle and Daubs, 2021), and YouTube's integration shopping features (Ørmen and Gregersen, 2022). All of these innovations are about the facilitation of direct economic transactions, either in terms of linking advertising and point-of-purchase or peer-to-peer transactions.

The explosive growth of alternative financial technologies can to some degree be seen as a consequence of the financial crisis, which weakened the authority of the two-tiered banking system (Hütten and Thiemann, 2017) and a revival of old utopias with regard to the governance of money (Eich, 2019). However, it is also a consequence of innovations in the field of peer-to-peer transactions, mobile money networks, and new markets in Africa (Kendall et al, 2011; Maurer, 2012) and established platform attempts to diversify into this field as well (Manzerolle and Wiseman, 2016; Manzerolle and Daubs, 2021). In their work on the transactional ecosystems of digital media, Manzerolle and Wiseman address how the commercial development of digital media is now blending with an emerging payment ecosystem. They argue that 'the development of mobile and ubiquitous payment platforms and capabilities will mature alongside media industry attempts to better measure and "monetize" attention' (2016: 393). In their article, they point out that media and commerce have evolved in mutual connection since the ancient times of Babylon, and they state that 'the means of communication and commerce, of payment and attention, is increasingly wedded together in the same device or platform' (2016: 395). While they do not consider this to be a 'fait accompli', platforms' efforts to embed market relations into the technologies and practices of digital media have potentially grave implications for the future media environment. In a later work, Manzerolle and Daubs define these efforts as a commercial interest 'to link advertising and point-of-purchase' (2021: 1281), and demonstrate this tendency by addressing, on one hand, the increasing 'monetization of authenticity' among social media influencers and, on the other, increasing efforts to integrate transaction affordances such as 'check out on Instagram' and 'Snapchat scan' in the same media. Transactional affordances in this context are defined as 'how the technical features enabling an economic exchange are realized through the contextual awareness and opportunities for specific types of action afforded to individual users' (2021: 1281). In a similar vein, Ørmen and Gregersen (2022) demonstrate how YouTube's business model is changing from the attention economy to the engagement economy, monetizing the interaction between the key actors on the platform: users, brands, and producers. While the relation between users and brands is monetized through the predominant model of advertising, YouTube also monetizes the relationship between producers and brands by facilitating sponsorships, producers, and users by integrating shopping features directly into its interface.

Lana Schwartz emphasizes the contemporary convergence of social media and payment technologies and how this indicates peer-to-peer transactions as a next step in digital platforms' business models: 'In recent years, the payments industry is shifting from Wall Street to Silicon Valley, from financial services to social media' (2020: 20). Her focus is on the convergence between social media and peer-to-peer transactions, and how this platform-based payment system differs from earlier institutional arrangements between merchants, banks, and independent sales organizations. New platform-based payment systems, she points out, keep users' money inside their closed loops for as long as possible and can, in this way, 'charge fees from users without paying out fees to external systems' (2020: 90), a very lucrative business model that several platforms are looking towards. In fact, Chinese platform Alibaba's expansion into peer-to-peer transactions and micro-loans and its growing significance as a key infrastructure for personal finance in China (Yuan and Zhang, forthcoming) may be one important reason behind the Chinese state's 'attack on tech' (*The Economist*) in 2021, right before the ANT group, the company behind Alibaba's financial services, embarked on its 'first public offering' in the global stock market. While the story was accompanied with relatively stereotypical imagery of communist workers hammering down on big market actors, it is not surprising that a state is reluctant to let the personal finances of its citizens and the infrastructures that undergird them depend on the whims of global stock markets (indeed, recollecting the 2007 financial crisis, they ought to be).

In short, the growth of fintech is not limited to blockchain, cryptocurrencies, and cryptocurrency exchange platforms, even though these phenomena certainly have gained increased significance (and notoriety) during recent times. Fintech also covers the more general innovations in terms of facilitating economic transactions between peers and between customers and merchants, and digital platforms have already started to make inroads into this domain. From this perspective, Steam's particular take on microtransactions and player trading and their potential development into an alternative instrument of payment is not just an exotic story from the strange lands of gaming, it may well indicate a general trend in Big Tech to be taken seriously. Steam is simultaneously a 'critical case' differing significantly from comparable platforms and a possible indication of things to come in the big platform business. The implications of this development are multifarious and significant, and in the conclusion of this book, I would bring up two points: the expansion of commodification into new domains of everyday life, and the importance of looking beyond personal data when regulating these emergent business models.

As concerns the first, my analysis in Chapter 5 demonstrates how the Steam platform converts affective value into market value by reorganizing the economic interaction of player-driven economies and gaming communities into market interaction through a process of 'dispossession by disembedment'. The domain of gaming lends itself particularly well to this business model due to the inherently economic nature of particular types of gameplay. However, several other domains of everyday and public life such as householding, public administration, and, indeed, democratic processes can similarly be reorganized as market interactions for commercial purposes, further intensifying commodification beyond the well-known domains of commercial popular culture and consumer product branding. Close attention should be paid to these expansive processes of commodification, including the possible implications for the domains in question, which leads me to my second point. Contemporary critiques of datafication and commodification processes on digital platforms tend to focus on the collection of personal data for the purposes of advertising, and so do regulatory frameworks. This does not mean that they are irrelevant. In a European perspective, GDPR and the digital services act are important and necessary measures in terms of protecting citizens and their personal data in the digital age. However, with their emphasis on personal data, they do not really address the issues raised by the business model of the Steam platform and other platforms' development towards personal finance. The simultaneous positioning of users as content providers and economic actors within a tangled market, and the emergence of informal monetary networks where potentially large sums change hands, mean that platforms as tangled markets should not just be obligated to protect users' data and use them inappropriately, but also protect users in their capacities as consumers, producers, and economic actors.

Notes

Chapter 1

1. www.espn.com/espn/feature/story/_/id/18510975/how-counter-strike-turned-teena
ger-compulsive-gambler
2. www.gamesindustry.biz/valve-threatened-with-legal-action-by-washington-state-gambl
ing-commission
3. https://partner.steamgames.com/doc/store/pricing
4. https://partner.steamgames.com/doc/features/microtransactions/implementation
5. https://cand.uscourts.gov/cases-e-filing/cases-of-interest/epic-games-inc-v-apple-inc

Chapter 2

1. www.isfe.eu/DATA-KEY-FACTS/KEY-FACTS-ABOUT-EUROPE-S-VIDEO-
GAMES-SECTOR

Chapter 3

1. Interestingly, Kokuryoo defines this managerial practice as a 'non-keiretsu-based'
system (Steinberg, 2019: 114), that is, an alternative to the vertically and horizontally
integrated groupings of firms, sometimes addressed as a distinctively Japanese way of
organizing markets in economic-sociological literature on markets (see Fligstein, 2001;
Granovetter, 2017).
2. Granovetter features a somewhat more precise version of this classic citation: 'The tone
was set by Adam Smith, who postulated a "certain propensity in human nature ... to
truck, barter and exchange one thing for another" ([1776] 1979, book 1, chapter 2)'
(Granovetter, 1985: 482).
3. Commodities and commodification are also key concepts in Marxist thought, to which
Polanyi was sympathetic, yet also sceptical. Polanyi's framework does not pay much
attention to class and does not provide a general theory of capitalism, which has led
to substantial critiques among contemporary Marxist thinkers such as Selwyn and
Miyamura (2014). As Richard Sandbrook (2015) suggests in a blog post, this scepticism
may be due to the 'economistic fallacies' of liberalism and Marxism that presume all
human action to be motivated by the economy, a viewpoint that Polanyi did not share.

Chapter 4

1. www.gamesradar.com/history-of-valve/
2. www.gamespot.com/articles/greatest-games-of-all-time-half-life/1100-6171044/
3. Gabe Newell makes this statement in an 'interactive storybook' published by Geoff
Keighley on the Steam platform. https://store.steampowered.com/app/1361700/Hal
fLife_Alyx__Final_Hours/

[4]   In fact, he stated that 'Windows 8 is a catastrophe for everyone in the PC space' at the Casual Connect game conference in Seattle in 2012. www.bbc.com/news/technology-18996377

[5]   Gabe Newell made this statement at the LinuxCon held in New Orleans in 2013. www.pcgamer.com/gabe-newell-linux-and-open-source-are-the-future-of-gaming

[6]   www.forbes.com/forbes/2011/0228/technology-gabe-newell-videogames-valve-online-mayhem.html?sh=4cc957c93ac0

[7]   www.forbes.com/forbes/2011/0228/technology-gabe-newell-videogames-valve-online-mayhem.html?sh=2b821c53ac0b

[8]   www.forbes.com/profile/gabe-newell/?sh=351658087da0

[9]   https://comparecamp.com/steam-statistics

[10] www.pcgamer.com/ea-games-are-coming-to-steam-starting-with-star-wars-jedi-fallen-order

[11] www.gamesindustry.biz/articles/2018-12-04-epic-launching-store-with-88-percent-revenue-share-for-developers

[12] www.theverge.com/2022/1/18/22889258/microsoft-activision-blizzard-xbox-acquisition-call-of-duty-overwatch

[13] Steam press release, 21 March 2002.

[14] www.gamesradar.com/history-of-valve

[15] www.valvesoftware.com/en/about

[16] http://wayback.archive.org

Chapter 5

[1]   Steam press release, 21 March 2002.

[2]   https://financesonline.com/steam-statistics

[3]   https://store.steampowered.com/oldnews/1574

[4]   https://store.steampowered.com/oldnews/8761

[5]   www.eurogamer.net/articles/2017-02-10-valve-is-removing-steam-greenlight-this-spring

[6]   https://store.steampowered.com/oldnews/16509

[7]   https://store.steampowered.com/oldnews/16509

Chapter 6

[1]   https://partner.steamgames.com/doc/store/pricing

[2]   https://partner.steamgames.com/doc/features/microtransactions/implementation

[3]   www.theverge.com/2019/4/16/18334865/epic-games-store-versus-steam-valve-pc-gaming-console-war-reimagined

[4]   www.theverge.com/2018/11/30/18120577/valve-steam-game-marketplace-revenue-split-new-rules-competition

[5]   https://help.steampowered.com/en/faqs/view/61F0-72B7-9A18-C70B#steamfee

Chapter 7

[1]   https://api.steampowered.com/ISteamApps/GetAppList/v2/

[2]   https://store.steampowered.com/api/appdetails?appids=

[3]   The current analysis is based on two dates in June 2021, but there were plans to create a more updated dataset during spring 2022.

[4]   https://api.steampowered.com/ISteamUserStats/GetNumberOfCurrentPlayers/v1/?format=json&appid=

[5]   www.isfe.eu/data-key-facts/key-facts-about-europe-s-video-games-sector

[6]   https://newzoo.com/resources/rankings/top-25-companies-game-revenues

Chapter 8

[1] https://store.steampowered.com/subscriber_agreement

[2] https://partner.steamgames.com/doc/features/microtransactions/implementation

[3] https://help.steampowered.com/en/faqs/view/18A5-167F-C27B-64A0

[4] www.juniperresearch.com/press/loot-boxes-and-skins-gambling

[5] https://help.steampowered.com/en/faqs/view/61F0-72B7-9A18-C70B#steamfee

[6] https://partner.steamgames.com/doc/features/microtransactions/implementation#7

[7] https://csgoskins.gg/markets

Chapter 9

[1] Walter Benjamin, who belonged to the same school of thought, offered a somewhat more nuanced perspective on this dichotomy (Benjamin, 1935).

References

Altice, N. (2015) *I Am Error: The Nintendo Family Computer/Entertainment System Platform*. MIT Press.

Andrejevic, M. (2011) The work that affective economics does. *Cultural Studies* 25(4–5): 604–20.

Arvidsson, A. (2006) Brand value. *Journal of Brand Management* 13: 188–92.

Aspers, P. (2011) *Markets*. Polity.

Banks, J. (2013) *Co-Creating Videogames*. Bloomsbury Publishing.

Baym, N.K. (2021) *Creator Culture: An Introduction to Global Social Media Entertainment*. NYU Press.

Beckert, J. (2007) The great transformation of embeddedness: Karl Polanyi and the new economic sociology. *MPIfG Discussion Paper 07/1* 38–55.

Beckert, J. (2009) The social order of markets. *Theory and Society* 38(3): 245–69. DOI: 10.1007/s11186-008-9082-0.

Benjamin, W. (1935) *The Work of Art in the Age of Mechanical Reproduction*.

Bjerg, O. (2016) How is Bitcoin money? *Theory, Culture & Society* 33(1): 53–72.

Bogost, I., and Montfort, N. (2009) 'Platform studies: frequently questioned answers'. Conference proceedings from the Digitaals Arts and Culture conference in Irvine, California, December 2009.

Boluk, S., and LeMieux, P. (2017) *Metagaming: Playing, Competing, Spectating, Cheating, Trading, Making, and Breaking Videogames*. University of Minnesota Press.

Brock, T., and Johnson, M. (2021) The gamblification of digital games. *Journal of Consumer Culture* 21(1): 3–13.

Bruns, A. (2008) *Blogs, Wikipedia, Second Life, and beyond: From Production to Produsage*. Peter Lang.

Burgess, J. (2021) Platform studies. In: Cunningham, S., and Craig, D. (eds) *Creator Culture: An Introduction to Global Social Media Entertainment*. New York University Press: pp 21–38.

Caraway, B. (2011) Audience labor in the new media environment: A Marxian revisiting of the audience commodity. *Media, Culture & Society* 33(5): 693–708.

Cassidy, R. (2013). Partial convergence: social gaming and real-money gambling. In: *Qualitative research in gambling*. Routledge: pp 74–91.

Castronova, E. (2001) Virtual worlds: a first-hand account of market and society on the cyberian frontier. Available at: SSRN 294828.

Castronova, E. (2006) *Synthetic Worlds: The Business and Culture of Online Games*. University of Chicago Press.

Cusumano, M. (2010) Technology strategy and management: the evolution of platform thinking. *Communications of the ACM* 53(1): 32–4.

Davis, A., and Walsh, C. (2017) Distinguishing financialization from neoliberalism. *Theory, Culture & Society* 34(5–6): 27–51.

DeNardis, L. (2012) Hidden levers of internet control: an infrastructure-based theory of internet governance. *Information, Communication & Society* 15(5): 720–38.

DiMaggio, P.J., and Powell, W.W. (1983) The iron cage revisited: institutional isomorphism and collective rationality in organizational fields. *American Sociological Review* 48(2): 147–60. DOI: https://doi.org/10.2307/2095101.

Dodd, N. (1994) *The Sociology of Money: Economics, Reason & Contemporary Society*. Polity Press.

Dodd, N. (2005) Reinventing monies in Europe. *Economy and Society* 34(4): 558–83.

Dodd, N. (2018) The social life of Bitcoin. *Theory, Culture & Society* 35(3): 35–56.

Doyle, G. (2013) *Understanding Media Economics*. SAGE Publications.

Duffy, B.E., Poell, T., and Nieborg, D.B. (2019) Platform practices in the cultural industries: creativity, labor, and citizenship. *Social Media + Society* 5(4): 1–8.

The Economist (2021) 'China's attack on tech', 14–20 August.

Eich, S. (2019) Old utopias, new tax havens: the politics of Bitcoin in historical perspective. In: P. Hacker, I. Lianos, G. Dimitropoulos, and S. Eich (eds) *Regulating Blockchain: Techno-Social and Legal Challenges*. Oxford University Press: pp 85–98.

Eisenmann, T., Parker, G., and Van Alstyne, M.W. (2006) Strategies for two-sided markets. *Harvard Business Review* 84(10): 92.

Evans, D.S., and Schmalensee, R. (2016) *Matchmakers: The New Economics of Multi-Sided Platforms*. Harvard Business Review Press.

Fligstein, N. (1990) *The Transformation of Corporate Control*. Harvard University Press.

Fligstein, N. (1996) Markets as politics: a political-cultural approach to market institutions. *American Sociological Review* 61(4): 656–73. DOI: 10.2307/2096398.

Fligstein, N. (2001) *The Architecture of Markets*. Princeton University Press.

Fortunati, L. (1995) *The Arcane of Reproduction: Housework, Prostitution, Labor and Capital*. Autonomedia.

Fourcade, M., and Healy, K. (2017) Seeing like a market. *Socio-Economic Review* 15(1): 9–29. DOI: 10.1093/ser/mww033.

Fuchs, C. (2011) An alternative view of privacy on Facebook. *Information* 2(1): 140–65.

Fuchs, C. (2013) Critique of the political economy of informational capitalism and social media. In: C. Fuchs and M. Sandoval (eds) *Critique, Social Media and the Information Society*. Routledge: pp 63–77.

Fuchs, C. (2014) Dallas Smythe and audience labour today. In: C. Fuchs (eds) *Digital Labour and Karl Marx*. Routledge: pp 90–150.

Fuchs, C. (2021) *Social Media: A Critical Introduction*. SAGE Publications.

Garcia-Parpet, M.-F. (2007) The social construction of a perfect market. In: D. MacKenzie, F. Muniesa, and L. Siu (eds) *Do Economists Make Markets? On the Performativity of Economics*. Princeton University Press: pp 20–53.

Gawer, A. (2011) *Platforms, Markets and Innovation*. Edward Elgar Publishing.

Gerlitz, C., and Helmond, A. (2013) The like economy: social buttons and the data-intensive web. *New Media & Society* 15(8): 1348–65.

Gillespie, T. (2010) The politics of 'platforms'. *New Media & Society* 12(3): 347–64. DOI: 10.1177/1461444809342738.

Goldhaber, M.H. (1997) The attention economy and the net. *First Monday* 2(4).

Granovetter, M. (1985) Economic action and social structure: the problem of embeddedness. *American Journal of Sociology* 91(3): 481–510.

Granovetter, M. (2017) *Society and Economy: Framework and Principles*. Harvard University Press.

Hall, S. (1980) *Encoding/Decoding in Culture, Media, Language*. Hutchinson.

Halman, J.I.M., Hofer, A.P., and Van Vuuren, W. (2003) Platform-driven development of product families: linking theory with practice. *Journal of Product Innovation Management* 20(2): 149–62.

Hamari, J., and Järvinen, A. (2011) Building customer relationship through game mechanics in social games. In: M.M. Cruz-Cunha, V.H. Varvalho, and P. Tavares (eds) *Business, Technological, and Social Dimensions of Computer Games: Multidisciplinary Developments*. IGI Global: pp 348–65.

Hamari, J., and Lehdonvirta, V. (2010) Game design as marketing: how game mechanics create demand for virtual goods. *International Journal of Business Science & Applied Management* 5(1): 14–29.

Hamari, J., Alha, K., Järvelä, S., Kivikangas, J.M., Koivisto, J., and Paavilainen, J. (2017) Why do players buy in-game content? An empirical study on concrete purchase motivations. *Computers in Human Behavior* 68: 538–46.

Harvey, D. (2005) *The New Imperialism*. Oxford University Press.

Helmond, A. (2015) The platformization of the web: making web data platform ready. *Social Media + Society* 1(2): 1–11.

Hermann, C. (2021) *The Critique of Commodification: Contours of a Post-Capitalist Society*. Oxford University Press.

Hills, M. (2003) *Fan Cultures*. Routledge.

Hoofnagle, C.J., and Whittington, J. (2013) Free: accounting for the costs of the internet's most popular price. *UCLA Law Review* 61: 606–671.

Horkheimer, M., and Adorno, T.W. (1972) *Dialectic of Enlightenment: Max Horkheimer and Theodor W. Adorono*. Seabury Press.

Horkheimer, M., and Adorno, T.W. (1973) *Dialektik der Aufklärung: philosophische Fragmente*. Fischer.

Hutchby, I. (2001) Technologies, texts and affordances. *Sociology* 35(2): 441–56.

Hütten, M., and Thiemann, M. (2017) Moneys at the margins: from political experiment to cashless societies. In: M. Campbell-Verduyn (ed) *Bitcoin and Beyond*. Routledge: pp 25–47.

Ingham, G. (2004) The nature of money. *Economic Sociology: European Electronic Newsletter* 5(2): 18–28.

Ingham, G. (2013) *The Nature of Money*. John Wiley & Sons.

Jarrett, J. (2021) Gaming the gift: the affective economy of League of Legends 'fair' free-to-play model. *Journal of Consumer Culture* 21(1): 102–19.

Jarrett, K. (2016) *Feminism, Labour and Digital Media: The Digital Housewife*. Routledge.

Jenkins, H. (2006) *Fans, Bloggers, and Gamers: Exploring Participatory Culture*. New York University Press. Available at: www.loc.gov/catdir/toc/ecip0 610/2006008890.html.

Jöckel, S., Will, A., and Schwarzer, F. (2008) Participatory media culture and digital online distribution – reconfiguring the value chain in the computer game industry. *The International Journal on Media Management* 10(3): 102–11.

Johnson, M.R., and Brock, T. (2020) The 'gambling turn' in digital game monetization. *Journal of Gaming & Virtual Worlds* 12(2): 145–63.

Jones, S.E., and Thiruvathukal, G.K. (2012) *Codename Revolution: The Nintendo Wii Platform*. MIT Press.

Joseph, D. (2017) Distributing productive play: a materialist analysis of Steam. Toronto Metropolitan University. Thesis. Available at: https://doi.org/10.32920/ryerson.14654079.v1

Joseph, D. (2021) Battle pass capitalism. *Journal of Consumer Culture* 21(1): 68–83.

Joseph, D.J. (2018) The discourse of digital dispossession: paid modifications and community crisis on steam. *Games and Culture* 13(7): 690–707.

Juul, J. (2010) *A Casual Revolution: Reinventing Video Games and their Players*. MIT Press.

Kendall, J., Machoka, P., Veniard, C., and Maurer, B. (2011) An emerging platform: from money transfer system to mobile money ecosystem. UC Irvine School of Law Research Paper.

Kenney, M., and Zysman, J. (2020) The platform economy: restructuring the space of capitalist accumulation. *Cambridge Journal of Regions, Economy and Society* 13(1): 55–76.

Kerr, A. (2017) *Global Games: Production, Circulation and Policy in the Networked Era.* Routledge.

Kerr, A. (2021) *The Circulation Game: Shifting Production Logics and Circulation Moments in the Digital Games Industry.* New York University.

Kim, J., and Min, J. (2019) Supplier, tailor, and facilitator: Typology of platform business models. *Journal of Open Innovation: Technology, Market, and Complexity* 5(3).

Kovach, S. (2021) Here's how Zuckerberg thinks Facebook will profit by building a 'metaverse'. *CNBC.* Online. Available at: https://www.cnbc.com/2021/07/29/facebook-metaverse-plans-to-make-money.html.

Kowert, R., Breuer, J., and Quandt, T. (2017) Women are from FarmVille, men are from ViceCity: The cycle of exclusion and sexism in video game content and culture. In: R. Kowert and T. Quandt (eds) *New Perspectives on the Social Aspects of Digital Gaming.* Routledge: pp 136–50.

Krippner, G.R. (2001) The elusive market: embeddedness and the paradigm of economic sociology. *Theory and Society* 30(6): 775–810.

Krippner, G.R., and Alvarez, A.S. (2007) Embeddedness and the intellectual projects of economic sociology. *Annual Review of Sociology* 33: 219–40.

Kücklich, J. (2005) Precarious playbour: modders and the digital games industry. *Fibreculture* 5(1): 1–5.

Langley, P., and Leyshon, A. (2017) Platform capitalism: the intermediation and capitalisation of digital economic circulation. *Finance and Society* 3(1): 11–31.

Lehdonvirta, V., and Castronova, E. (2014) *Virtual Economies: Design and Analysis.* MIT Press.

Lessig, L. (2006) *Code: And Other Laws of Cyberspace, Version 2.0.* Basic Books.

Lewis, C., Wardrip-Fruin, N., and Whitehead, J. (2012) Motivational game design patterns of 'ville games. In: *Proceedings of the International Conference on the Foundations of Digital Games.* ACM: pp 172–79.

Light, B., Burgess, J., and Duguay, S. (2018) The walkthrough method: an approach to the study of apps. *New Media & Society* 20(3): 881–900.

Macey, J., and Hamari, J. (2022) Gamblification: A definition. *New Media & Society* (0). DOI: 10.1177/1461444822108390.

MacKenzie, D. (2018) 'Making', 'taking' and the material political economy of algorithmic trading. *Economy and Society* 47(4): 501–23.

Manzerolle, V. (2010) Mobilizing the audience commodity: digital labour in a wireless world. *Ephemera: Theory & Politics in Organization* 10(4): 455.

Manzerolle, V., and Daubs, M. (2021) Friction-free authenticity: mobile social networks and transactional affordances. *Media, Culture & Society* 43(7): 1279–96.

Manzerolle, V., and Wiseman, A. (2016) On the transactional ecosystems of digital media. *Communication and the Public* 1(4): 393–408.

Maurer, B. (2012) Mobile money: communication, consumption and change in the payments space. *Journal of Development Studies* 48(5): 589–604.

Miège, B. (1987) The logics at work in the new cultural industries. *Media, Culture & Society* 9(3): 273–89.

Montfort, N., and Bogost, I. (2009) *Racing the Beam: The Atari Video Computer System.* MIT Press.

Murji, K. (2007) Hierarchies, markets and networks: ethnicity/race and drug distribution. *Journal of Drug Issues* 37(4): 781–804.

Nieborg, D.B. (2015) Crushing candy: the free-to-play game in its connective commodity form. *Social Media + Society* 1(2): 1–12.

Nieborg, D.B. (2016) Free-to-play games and app advertising: the rise of the player commodity. In: J.F. Hamilton, R. Bodle, and E. Korin (eds) *Explorations in Critical Studies of Advertising.* Routledge: pp 38–51.

Nieborg, D.B. (2021) Apps of empire: Global capitalism and the app economy. *Games and Culture* 16(3): 305–16.

Nieborg, D.B., and Poell, T. (2018) The platformization of cultural production: theorizing the contingent cultural commodity. *New Media & Society* 20(11): 4275–92.

Nielsen, R.K.L., and Grabarczyk, P. (2019) *Are Loot Boxes Gambling? Random Reward Mechanisms in Video Games.* DIGRA.

O'Reilly, T. (2007) What is Web 2.0: design patterns and business models for the next generation of software. *Communications & Strategies* 1: 17.

Ørmen, J., and Gregersen, A. (2022) Towards the engagement economy: interconnected processes of commodification on YouTube. *Media, Culture & Society* 45(2): 225–45.

Parker, G.G., Van Alstyne, M.W., and Choudary, S.P. (2016) *Platform Revolution: How Networked Markets are Transforming the Economy and How to Make them Work for You.* WW Norton & Company.

Peck, J. (2013) Disembedding Polanyi: exploring Polanyian economic geographies. *Environment and Planning A* 45(7): 1536–44.

Peck, J., and Phillips, R. (2020) The platform conjuncture. *Sociologica* 14(3): 73–99.

Pfeffer, J., and Salancik, G.R. (2003) *The External Control of Organizations: A Resource Dependence Perspective.* Stanford University Press.

Plantin, J.-C., and Punathambekar, A. (2019) Digital media infrastructures: pipes, platforms, and politics. *Media, Culture & Society* 41(2): 163–74.

Poell, T., Nieborg, D., and Van Dijck, J. (2019) Platformisation. *Internet Policy Review* 8(4): 1–13.

Polanyi, K. (1944) *The Great Transformation.* Beacon Press.

Poole, S. (2000) *Trigger Happy: Videogames and the Entertainment Revolution.* Arcade Publishing.

Postigo, H. (2007) Of mods and modders: chasing down the value of fan-based digital game modifications. *Games and Culture* 2(4): 300–13.

Ritzer, G., and Jurgenson, N. (2010) Production, consumption, prosumption: the nature of capitalism in the age of the digital 'prosumer'. *Journal of Consumer Culture* 10(1): 13–36.

Rochet, J.-C., and Tirole, J. (2003) Platform competition in two-sided markets. *Journal of the European Economic Association* 1(4): 990–1029.

Samuelson, P. (1973) *Economics*, 9th ed. McGraw-Hill.

Sandbrook, R. (2015) Why Polanyi and not Marx? Blog. Available at: https://sandbroo.faculty.politics.utoronto.ca/why-polanyi-and-not-marx/

Selwyn, B. and Miyamura, S. (2014) Class struggle or embedded markets? Marx, Polanyi and the meanings and possibilities of social transformation. *New Political Economy* 19(5): 639–661.

Smythe, D.W. (1981) On the audience commodity and its work. In: M.G. Durham and D.M. Kellner (eds) *Media and Cultural Studies: Keyworks*. Blackwell: pp 230–56.

Søraker, J.H. (2016) Gaming the gamer? The ethics of exploiting psychological research in video games. *Journal of Information, Communication and Ethics in Society* 14(2): 106–23.

Sparsam, J. (2016) Understanding the 'economic' in new economic sociology. *Economic Sociology: The European Electronic Newsletter* 18(1): 6–17.

Srnicek, N. (2017) *Platform Capitalism*. John Wiley & Sons.

Stark, D., and Pais, I. (2020) Algorithmic management in the platform economy. *Sociologica* 14(3): 47–72.

Steinberg, M. (2019) *The Platform Economy: How Japan Transformed the Consumer Internet*. University of Minnesota Press.

Stone, B. (2013) *The Everything Store: Jeff Bezos and the Age of Amazon*. Random House.

Swartz, L. (2020) *New Money*. Yale University Press.

Taplin, J. (2017) *Move Fast and Break Things: How Facebook, Google, and Amazon have Cornered Culture and What it Means for All of Us*. Pan Macmillan.

Terranova, T. (2000) Free labor: producing culture for the digital economy. *Social Text* 18(2): 33–58.

Terranova, T. (2003) Free labor: producing culture for the digital economy – Tiziana Terranova. Available at: www.electronicbookreview.com/thread/technocapitalism/voluntary

Thorhauge, A.M. (2022) The steam platform economy: from retail to player-driven economies. *New Media & Society*. DOI: https://doi.org/10.1177/14614448221081401

Thorhauge, A.M (2024) Player-driven economies and money at the margins. In: A.M. Thorhauge, A. Gregersen, J. Ørmen, E.I. Otto, and M.A. Pedersen (eds) *The Economic Lives of Platforms*. Bristol University Press.

Thorhauge, A.M., and Nielsen, R.K.L. (2021) Epic, Steam and the role of skin-betting in game (platform) economies. *Consumer Culture* 21(1): 52–67.

Tubaro, P. (2021) Disembedded or deeply embedded? A multi-level network analysis of online labour platforms. *Sociology* 55(5): 927–44.

Van Couvering, E. (2011) Navigational media: the political economy of online traffic. In: D.W. Dal Yong Jin (ed) *The Political Economics of Media: The Transformation of the Global Media Industries.* Bloomsbury Academic: pp 183–200.

Van Dijck, J. (2013) *The Culture of Connectivity: A Critical History of Social Media.* Oxford University Press.

Van Dijck, J., Poell, T., and De Waal, M. (2018) *The Platform Society: Public Values in a Connective World.* Oxford University Press.

Vogel, S.K. (2018) *Marketcraft: How Governments Make Markets Work.* Oxford University Press.

Vonderau, P. (2019) The Spotify effect: digital distribution and financial growth. *Television & New Media* 20(1): 3–19.

Wallerstein, I. (1983) *Historical Capitalism.* Verso.

Weber, D. (2021) Exploring markets: Magic the gathering – a trading card game. IUBH Discussion Papers – Business & Management.

Webster, J.G. (2014) *The Marketplace of Attention: How Audiences Take Shape in a Digital Age.* MIT Press.

Werning, S. (2019) Disrupting video game distribution: a diachronic affordance analysis of Steam's platformization strategy. *Nordic Journal of Media Studies* 1(1): 103–24.

White, H.C. (1981) Where do markets come from? *American Journal of Sociology* 87(3): 517–47.

White, H.C. (2002) *Markets from Networks.* Princeton University Press.

Williamson, O.E. (1973) Markets and hierarchies: some elementary considerations. *The American Economic Review* 63(2): 316–25.

Wrong, D.H. (1963) The oversocialized conception of man in modern sociology. In: N.J. Smelser and W.T. Smelser (eds) *Personality and Social Systems.* John Wiley & Sons: pp 68–79. Available at: https://doi.org/10.1037/11302-004

Xiao, L.Y., Henderson, L.L., Nielsen, R.K.L., Grabarczyk, P., Newall, P.W., and Lee, N. (2021) Loot boxes, gambling-like mechanics in video games. In: *Encyclopedia of Computer Graphics and Games.* Springer: np.

Zanescu, A., French, M., and Lajeunesse, M. (2020) Betting on DOTA 2's Battle Pass: gamblification and productivity in play. *New Media & Society,* 23(10): 2882–901. DOI: 10.1177/1461444820941381.

Zanescu, A., Lajeunesse, M., and French, M. (2021) Speculating on Steam: consumption in the gamblified platform ecosystem. *Journal of Consumer Culture* 21(1): 34–51.

Zuboff, S. (2015) Big other: surveillance capitalism and the prospects of an information civilization. *Journal of Information Technology* 30(1): 75–89.

Zuboff, S. (2019) *The Age of Surveillance Capitalism: The Fight for a Human Future at the New Frontier of Power.* Profile Books.

Games

343 Industries (2021) *Halo Infinite*. Digital game distributed by Xbox Game Studios.

Bethesda Game Studios (2011) *The Elder Scrolls V: Skyrim*. Digital game distributed by Bethesda Softworks.

Blizzard Entertainment (2004) *World of Warcraft*. Digital game distributed by Blizzard Entertainment.

Epic Games (2017) *Fortnite*. Digital game distributed by Epic Games.

Facepunch Studios and Double Eleven (2018) *Rust*. Digital game distributed by Facepunch Studios.

Garfield, R. (1993) *Magic: The Gathering*. Card game distributed by Wizards of the Coast.

Guerrilla Games (2017) *Horizon Zero Dawn*. Digital game distributed by Sony Interactive Entertainment.

Iisalo, Jakko (2009) *Angry Birds*. Digital game distributed by Rovio Entertainment.

King (2012) *Candy Crush Saga*. Digital game distributed by King.

Mojang Studios (2011) *Minecraft*. Digital game distributed by Mojang Studios, Xbox Game Studios and Sony Interactive Entertainment.

Psyonix (2015) *Rocket League*. Digital game distributed by Psyonix.

PUBG studios (2017) *PlayerUnknown's Battlegrounds*. Digital game distributed by Krafton, Microsoft Studios and Tencent Games.

Respawn Entertainment (2019) *Apex Legends*. Digital game distributed by Electronic Arts.

Riot Games (2013) *League of Legends*. Digital game distributed by Riot Games.

Roblox Corporation (2006) *Roblox*. Game platform owned by Roblox Corporation.

TML Team (2020) *tMODloader*. Modification of *Terraria* (Re-Logic, 2011) distributed by Re-Logic and TML Team.

Valve (2000) *Counter-Strike*. Half-Life modification developed by Minh Le and Jess Cliffe. Distributed by Sierra Studies and Valve.

Valve (2007) *Team Fortress 2*. Digital game distributed by Valve.

Valve (2013) *Dota 2*. Digital game distributed by Valve.

Valve (2018) *Artifact*. Digital game distributed by Valve.

Valve (2020) *Half-Life: Alyx*. Digital game distributed by Valve.

Valve and Gearbox Software (1998) *Half-Life*. Digital game distributed by Sierra online and Valve.

Valve and Hidden Path Entertainment (2012) *Counter-Strike: Global Offensive*. Digital game distributed by Valve.

Verant Interactive and 989 Studios (1999) *Everquest*. Digital game distributed by Sony Entertainment and Ubisoft.

VRChat Inc. (2017) *VRChat*. Virtual Wordl distributed by VRChat Inc.

Index

References to figures appear in *italic* type;
those in **bold** type refer to tables.